GREAT WRITERS STUDENT LIBRARY

THE BEGINNINGS
TO 1558

GREAT WRITERS STUDENT LIBRARY

Editor: James Vinson
Associate Editor: D. L. Kirkpatrick

GREAT WRITERS STUDENT LIBRARY

THE BEGINNINGS
TO 1558

INTRODUCTION BY
ALLAN H. MacLAINE

First published 1980 by
THE MACMILLAN PRESS LIMITED
London and Basingstoke
Associated companies in New York, Dublin
Melbourne, Johannesburg and Madras

ISBN 0333 28344 9

CONTENTS

EDITOR'S NOTE

The entry for each writer consists of a biography, a complete list of his published books, a selected list of published bibliographies and critical studies on the writer, and a signed critical essay on his work.

In the biographies, details of education, military service, and marriage(s) are generally given before the usual chronological summary of the life of the writer; awards and honours are given last.

The Publications section is meant to include all book publications, though as a rule broadsheets, single sermons and lectures, minor pamphlets, exhibition catalogues, etc. are omitted. Under the heading Collections, we have listed the most recent collections of the complete works and those of individual genres (verse, plays, novels, stories, and letters); only those collections which have some editorial authority and were issued after the writer's death are listed; on-going editions are indicated by a dash after the date of publication; often a general selection from the writer's works or a selection from the works in the individual genres listed above is included.

Titles are given in modern spelling, though the essayists were allowed to use original spelling for titles and quotations; often the titles are "short." The date given is that of the first book publication, which often followed the first periodical or anthology publication by some time; we have listed the actual year of publication, often different from that given on the title-page. No attempt has been made to indicate which works were published anonymously or pseudonymously, or which works of fiction were published in more than one volume, or to list lost or unverified plays. Reprints of books (including facsimile editions) and revivals of plays are not listed unless a revision or change of title is involved. The most recent edited version of individual works is included if it supersedes the collected edition cited.

In the essays, short references to critical remarks refer to items cited in the Publications section or in the Reading List. Introductions, memoirs, editorial matter, etc. in works cited in the Publications section are not repeated in the Reading List.

INTRODUCTION

The scope of this essay, and of the volume as a whole, is limited in two important respects. In the first place, we are concerned here with what might be called "creative" literature only, and have deliberately excluded the very large bulk of writings in the Old English, Middle English, and Early Tudor periods that are purely didactic or utilitarian in purpose. Works of the latter kind are included only in the few instances (such as *The Dream of the Rood* or *Pearl*) where the basic didactic aim is accompanied by a high degree of literary artistry and originality. This is a line which is often difficult to draw, but the emphasis throughout is upon literature as art. A second limitation arises from the fact that a very sizable proportion of our early literature, especially that in Old and Middle English, is the work of anonymous writers and cannot easily be represented by author entries in this volume. It would be impossible, for instance, to have "author" entries for the scores of folk ballads or anonymous lyric poems of high literary value. In fact, only three nameless authors of supreme importance are included in the body of the volume – the "*Beowulf* Poet," the "*Gawain* Poet," and "The Wakefield Master." As a consequence, this introductory essay attempts to fill in the unavoidable gaps by treating the anonymous literature of these periods in some detail, within a general summary of the whole.

Any attempt to survey a field as vast as this, extending over a time span of almost a thousand years and embracing many complex literary types and tendencies, necessarily calls for a considerable degree of organization and classification to make sense of it all. For the sake of order and clarity, therefore, I have adopted the traditional historical divisions into Old English, Middle English, and Early Tudor periods, together with some subdivisions by genre within each of these eras.

OLD ENGLISH LITERATURE

The earliest phase of our literature, written in the language called Old English or Anglo-Saxon, extends over an enormous stretch of time – approximately five hundred years – from the earliest surviving specimens dating from about 600 A.D. to the latest around 1100. Our knowledge of this literature and of the culture that produced it is extremely fragmentary. Only a small fraction of the writings in Old English have survived the hazards of fire, warfare, and natural disasters through the centuries. Indeed, *Beowulf*, the greatest monument of Old English literature, has come down to us only by a fortunate accident in a single, damaged manuscript, and the same is true of most of the rest. What has been lost we can only guess at.

Probably the earliest writing in England during these centuries was in Latin prose, brought in by the missionaries who converted the Anglo-Saxons to Christianity (c. 600–50); Latin continued to thrive as the language of the church and of learning throughout the Old English period and long afterwards. In the native tongue, as in all emergent cultures, poetry evolved first. Prose in Old English (much of which survives) was a much later development under the stimulus of King Alfred the Great (849–99). Virtually all of the prose writing, however, both in Latin and in Old English, was religious and didactic in purpose – partial translations of the Bible, saints' lives, homilies, histories, and so forth. The sole surviving great artistic achievement in prose during the entire five centuries, the Venerable Bede's magnificent *Ecclesiastical History of the English People* (731), was written in Latin and therefore falls outside the purview of this volume. Our focus here must be exclusively upon the nature and evolution of Old English Poetry.

In poetry, two distinct "golden ages" may be discerned in the Old English period, despite the incompleteness of records. The first of these developed in the north, in Northumbria and Mercia (the Midlands), reaching its climax shortly after 700. During the long, confused, Anglo-Saxon invasion of England (c. 450–600) several small independent kingdoms had been formed. The first of these to attain real stability and authority was Kent, where the Christian conversion of the English people began in 597. The balance of power soon shifted to the north, however, with the emergence of the Anglian kingdom of Northumbria about 625. Here, under a series of strong and brilliant kings, Northumbria rapidly developed not only a powerful political and military state, but also a flourishing monastic system and an amazingly sophisticated literary culture. The Northumbrian golden age produced the great scholar Bede, the *Beowulf* poet, the intrepid St. Cuthbert, and many other distinguished leaders in church and state. After the decline of Northumbria and then of Mercia in the latter part of the eighth century, the center of Anglo-Saxon culture moved back to the south with the gradual rise and final dominance of the kingdom of Wessex. The reign of King Alfred (871–99) ushered in a second golden age in English civilization which lasted through most of the next century.

Recent discoveries have drastically revised traditional views of Anglo-Saxon civilization before the Norman Conquest. The older conception was that England before the Conquest was inhabited by continuously warring tribes of mindless barbarians, beer-swilling bullies who managed to produce only occasional miraculous pockets of civilization during their centuries of dominance; and that the land was finally rescued from this long night of barbarism by the arrival of the Normans in 1066. This idea is now completely discredited. The discovery in 1939 at Sutton Hoo in Suffolk of a seventh-century burial ship containing splendid art treasures has helped to correct the earlier view. The superb bowls and spoons in the Sutton Hoo treasure prove that the English were in touch with Byzantine art even at this early date, and that their native crafts were among the most advanced in Europe. There can be no doubt, moreover, that Northumbria in the age of Bede was the most dynamic center of scholarship and literary culture in Northern Europe. The elaborate poetics of Old English verse, extending over the entire period, are also wholly inconsistent with the notion of a primitive culture.

It is true, of course, that the great mass of people in Anglo-Saxon England were illiterate; but that is also true of every area of Western Europe in that age. The arts of reading and writing were introduced by the Roman and Irish missionaries who brought in Christianity, beginning in 597; but literacy probably never extended much beyond the clergy and some of the aristocracy. One can conjecture that the literacy rate, even in the golden ages, never exceeded one percent of the population, if indeed it reached that. For that reason, all of the surviving literature in Old English is aristocratic in nature. It is also largely oral – the poetry is wholly so – that is, composed for oral performance before a listening audience, rather than for reading. But a culture that is mainly illiterate and a literature that is mainly oral are not necessarily crude or primitive. Old English poetry, on the contrary, is surprisingly sophisticated. The audience for which it was composed must have been highly skilled in the art of listening, an art which has been lost to the modern world since the spread of printing and mass education. Chaucer's audience, centuries later, and Shakespeare's too, must have been superb listeners. We are so used to the printed word today that it is difficult for us to imagine an oral culture wherein individuals trained themselves from childhood not in reading or writing but in listening to the *spoken* word with keen concentration, comprehension, and delight.

The audience for Anglo-Saxon poetry must have consisted of relatively cultivated people, not only skilled listeners but also steeped in the intricacies of a German poetic tradition that was already centuries old when it was brought across the North Sea into England from the Continental homelands. Our poetry, then, is only part of an international poetic tradition shared by all of the Germanic peoples of Northern Europe. Hence Beowulf, the hero of the greatest surviving poem in Old English, is not even an Englishman but the leader of a Scandinavian tribe. Clearly, the Germanic peoples of many lands shared a common mythology, a common religion, and a common literary heritage.

The depth and pervasiveness of this oral poetic tradition is attested by the astonishing fact that virtually all of the surviving poetry in Old English (about thirty thousand lines of it) is in the same basic verse form. The fundamental metrical unit is the half-line, containing two heavily stressed syllables and a varying number of lightly stressed or unaccented syllables arranged in any one of five standard sequences. In each full line the two half-lines are bridged by a pattern of alliteration which is the basic unifying device. With very few and minor exceptions Old English poetry is unrhymed; it is always alliterative. Within this rather difficult verse form, the diction and style of the poetry are notably formalized and sophisticated, far removed from the patterns of everyday speech that are observable in the simpler, more straightforward prose. Frequent use is made of traditional oral formulas of various kinds, familiar to both performer and audience. For the performer these formulas function as aids to memory; for the audience they provide a means of instant and easy identification of the person or thing described. Some of the formulas are simple patronymics, always prominent in tribal societies where blood relationships are crucial (Beowulf is "the son of Ecgtheow"); others are descriptive phrases defining a character's role (the king is "the noble lord" or "the giver of rings" or "the guardian of the people"); and so forth. Many of these oral formulaic phrases are similar to the "stock epithets" used in Homer's *Iliad* and *Odyssey,* and have similar functions and effects. A special kind of formula, unique to the Germanic tradition, is the *kenning.* This is an imaginative metaphor, sometimes bordering on the fantastic, used to depict a quite ordinary thing. The sea, for example, may be called "the whale's road" or "the gannett's bath"; a ship is a "wave cleaver." The most far-fetched of all the kennings in Old English poetry, I think, occurs in *Beowulf* where a sword is referred to as "the leavings of files," that is, what is left after the files have done their work!

The remarkable fact is that *all* of Old English poetry, no matter what its purpose or genre may be – whether it is heroic, or lyric, or elegiac, or religious, or didactic – is written in the same general style, with the same kind of diction, the same kind of elaborate oral formulas, the same complex verse form. And that fact is strong proof of how deeply entrenched the Germanic poetic tradition must have been in the minds of people of all classes. It should be noted, further, that it was in England that this tradition saw its earliest great flowering; in Scandinavia and in Germany comparable achievements did not evolve until centuries later.

How was Anglo-Saxon poetry actually presented? On this score there are many uncertainties, but a few facts are clear. Each cultural center – the headquarters of a tribe, the court of a king, the great hall of an important monastery – seems to have had a professional poet, a scop or bard (often, no doubt, more than one) who was both a composer in his own right and a performer of traditional works. The scop was certainly a man who was highly skilled and highly honored, usually a member of the aristocracy performing for an aristocratic audience. (The herdsman Caedmon, in Bede's account, was regarded as a kind of miracle because he was a common man who, by divine inspiration, suddenly attained the cultivated skills of a professional poet.) The scop's position may often have been hereditary, and after long years of training and practice he could spellbind his sophisticated audience with the power, beauty, and dramatic impact of his rendition. We know from Bede's story of Caedmon, from the passages in *Beowulf,* and from other sources that, at least in the earlier centuries, the scop accompanied himself on a harp. The partial remains of such a harp were found among the treasures at Sutton Hoo. But exactly how the music was matched to the words is unknown. It may be that various strums or glissades on the harp were used merely to punctuate the verse, so to speak, to indicate pauses, to build tempo, to preface dramatic moments; or the music may also have been played simultaneously with the speaking of the words. No one really knows. At any rate, it is clear that both the performance and the reception of Old English poetry must have been extremely cultivated: the power and brilliance of the scop were entrancing; the listening skill of the audience surpassed anything imaginable to modern ears.

A full appreciation of Old English poetry is now impossible, for two basic reasons. For one thing, we cannot duplicate either the kind of rendition for which the poems were composed or the kind of trained listening response they received. Secondly, there is the problem of the language itself. Old English is a difficult language, far more complex in its structure than modern English, comparable in grammatical intricacy to Latin. For modern English readers it is, in essence, and despite some common vocabulary, a foreign language that takes years of study to master. And even to expert readers of Old English, many of the subtle nuances so crucial to poetry are inaccessible. Nevertheless, a good deal of the special power and splendor of this poetry comes through to us, even in translation (and there are several excellent ones), after a thousand years. Despite all difficulties and inadequacies, it still retains a genuine interest, a unique fascination for readers in the late twentieth century.

Old English poetry has been classified according to genre in various ways, under such specialized rubrics as "Charms," "Riddles," "Elegies," and "Gnomic Verse." However, the great poetry, the poetry that counts as literary art, may easily be divided into three basic groupings, with some overlapping: (1) heroic, (2) lyric, and (3) religious.

Heroic Poetry

The bulk of Old English poetry is heroic in style and atmosphere, including most of the religious poems, as we shall see later. Our concern in this section, however, is limited to the poetry that is heroic in subject matter as well as style, the non-religious poetry that glorifies the warrior hero. In this genre there are some six extant pieces which may be listed in roughly chronological order as follows: *Widsith* (c. 675), *Waldere* (c. 750), *The Fight at Finnsburh* (c. 750), *Beowulf* (c.700–50), *The Battle of Brunanburh* (c. 937), and *The Battle of Maldon* (c. 991).

All of these poems, of course, are part of a general Germanic heroic tradition, a culture based upon the prowess of the warrior. In its earlier phases this culture was tribal. Each tribe, most of its members related to each other by blood, controlled a certain territory. The bulk of the tribal population would be common people – farmers, herdsmen, fishermen, a few craftsmen – whose work provided the economic foundations needed for survival. At the top, however, was a warrior aristocracy, consisting of a chieftain or a king surrounded by a *comitatus* of fighting men whose functions were to rule and to protect the tribe from hostile or predatory neighbors. In a world of frequent intertribal warfare, the fighting men were inevitably the ruling class. They dispensed justice and administered the resources of the tribe; they also defended the people from external enemies. The very survival of the tribe depended upon the courage and skill of this warrior aristocracy. The warrior class, consequently, was bound by a rigid traditional code of behavior. The first requirement was absolute loyalty to the king, to the general interests of the tribe, and to the welfare of every member in it. In this kind of society blood relationships and pride in ancestry were naturally of prime importance. The code also involved the duty to avenge the death or injury of any fellow tribesman at the hands of an outsider, and this rigid law led to endless blood feuds among the tribes. Sometimes the injury could be compensated by a payment of money (*wergild*), but more often bitter enmity resulted; the revenge motive was probably the main reason that the Germanic peoples were unable for centuries to achieve any kind of political unity. In such a violent and precarious world, then, it was only natural that the virtues of the warrior – courage, loyalty, physical strength, fighting skill, generosity, self-confidence – should be celebrated in poems and songs.

The Germanic heroic tradition in poetry thus rose inevitably out of these cultural conditions. The chief entertainment of the aristocracy (doubtless also of the common people on a simpler level) was to sit with their leader or king in the tribal headquarters and listen to the local scop performing exciting stories of past exploits of the tribe, exalting their heroic ancestors. *Widsith,* which is among the very earliest surviving writings in Old English, fits the pattern perfectly. In this brief poem (143 lines) the speaker is a fictional scop, Widsith ("far traveller"), a bard who has wandered from court to court over most of Germanic Europe. He celebrates his own marvelous skill and the honors he has received everywhere, and then goes on in the body of the poem to give three catalogues of famous Germanic heroes he has entertained in many lands, including the ancestor of the great Anglo-Saxon king, Offa of Mercia. The framework is fiction, since Widsith has played for heroic leaders known to have lived in actuality over a span of two centuries, but the poem as a whole is impressive for the insight it gives into the high dignity of the scop's status in early Germanic society, and interesting for its roll call of legendary names and exploits.

Waldere and *The Fight at Finnsburg* are two heroic fragments dating from the century after *Widsith* and roughly contemporaneous with *Beowulf. Waldere* consists mainly of two extended speeches which are fragments of what must have been a full-fledged epic (the surrounding story is known from the tenth-century Latin poem *Waltharius*). In the first speech the lady Hildeguth exhorts her lover Waldere to fight bravely in the coming duel with Guthhere; in the second Waldere challenges his opponent in a spirited "epic boast." *The Fight at Finnsburg* is another tempting fragment, as vigorous and exciting as *Waldere* in style, about a blood feud between the Danes and the Frisians, that is also treated in a major digression in *Beowulf* (the so-called "Lay of Finnsburg").

These brief heroic poems, however, are completely overshadowed by the massive and splendid epic of Beowulf, composed probably for the court of Northumbria about 700, or for that of Mercia around 750. Here we have the full panoply of the Germanic heroic tradition: the wise and gracious king Hrothgar in his magnificent mead hall, surrounded by a noble *comitatus* of Danish warriors, and visited by the even nobler band of heroic Geats led by Beowulf, the ideal Germanic hero; the sweet singing of the scop; the spirited challenges and epic boasts; the exciting and gruesome battles – the episodes (the fight with Grendel, for example) are recounted with fine narrative artistry and brilliant selection of detail. Similarly, the subtle fusion of brooding heathen fatalism with Christian philosophy is managed with great skill. There are many passages in *Beowulf,* such as Hrothgar's moving lament for Aeschere or the funeral scene, that show poetic art of a very high order – a special kind of profound, overwhelming eloquence. *Beowulf* is not only the longest surviving poem in the Old English language, it is also, by far, the best.

The four specimens of heroic verse we have just been considering share two things: they all belong to the early phase of Old English literature, the first golden age, and they all look back in their subject matter to a much earlier era of Germanic heroic legend. In contrast, the remaining two pieces of this genre, *The Battle of Brunanburh* and *The Battle of Maldon,* were composed some two centuries later, toward the end of the second peak in Old English culture, and they celebrate not the past but contemporaneous events. Both events have been recorded in the historical annals called *The Anglo-Saxon Chronicle* in entries for the years 937 and 991 respectively. Both poems are written in the heroic style, with the same difficult verse form, the same kind of elaborate aristocratic diction and oral formulas that are characteristic of *Beowulf* and the other early examples of this genre – a further evidence of the amazing depth and persistence of the Germanic oral tradition in poetry.

The Battle of Brunanburh has survived as a poetic entry in *The Anglo-Saxon Chronicle* itself, and it celebrates the victory of the English king Athelstan in a crucial battle against a combined army of Scots and Scandinavian forces, a battle that took place somewhere in the Northwest of England in the year 937. As a poem in the old alliterative style it is vigorous, effective, highly nationalistic, glorifying an important English victory. As literary art, however, it is surpassed by the truly great *Battle of Maldon.* This poem commemorates a minor local fight between the men of Essex under their heroic leader Bryhtnoth and a raiding band of Vikings in 991. In this case the English defenders are defeated and mostly slain, overwhelmed by superior force. The story is told as though by an eye witness to the actual battle, with powerful dramatic speeches, and the focus is on the tragic heroism of Bryhtnoth and his devoted men who refused to give ground in the face of certain death. The whole essence of the Germanic spirit, the ideals of courage and of loyalty of leader and countrymen, are brought vividly to life in this extraordinary work. *The Battle of Maldon,* only 325 lines long, is the finest heroic poem in Old English after *Beowulf.*

Lyric Poetry

Into this general class of Old English verse fall a number of short poems that are definitely lyrical in quality. There are, of course, many lyrical passages in *Beowulf* and in other heroic poems as well as in several religious poems; but we are concerned here with those pieces that are lyric poems in their entirety. Some seven or eight of these, all of uncertain date, have survived, of which three are masterpieces.

Among the lyrics of lesser importance, three are more or less love poems. *Wulf and Eadwacer* is the most impassioned of these, and presents a woman's anguished yearning for her lover who has been cruelly separated from her. *The Wife's Lament* expresses a woman's grief over the deliberate absence of her estranged husband. *The Husband's Message* gives us a man's eloquent entreaty to his wife to join him in a far country. It is a curious fact that love is an emotion rarely expressed in Anglo-Saxon poetry; these three minor lyrics are nearly all we have on the subject. One other piece that deserves mention here is *The Ruin,* a brief but fairly impressive fragment lamenting the desolation of the once splendid Roman city of Bath.

The three great surviving lyrics in Old English are *Deor, The Wanderer,* and *The Seafarer,* all of which are general "elegies," that is, poems expressing grief over the passing away of former happiness, beauty, or glory. *Deor* is remarkable, almost unique in Old English poetry, for the use of stanzas and a recurring refrain, in addition to the usual alliteration. The speaker is a scop (as in *Widsith*) who has been supplanted in his position by a talented rival, but this information is cleverly withheld until the end of the poem. In the first five stanzas, Deor tells of famous Germanic heroes and heroines who suffered disasters but were able to recover in some fashion, each stanza ending with the powerful refrain: "That grief was overcome; so may this be!" In the final stanza Deor reveals his own sad plight and ends on a note of stoic acceptance. The poem as a whole is aesthetically pleasing, eloquent, and moving.

The Wanderer is even better. This great lyric is the self-revelation and musings of an exiled nobleman who has lost his leader and warrior comrades (all killed) and must wander the earth as a man without a country. In tribal societies, in fact, to be cast adrift without the protection and fellowship of one's clan was a fate almost worse than death. The speaker, in the first part of this short poem (115 lines), retells the disaster that has befallen him and recalls poignantly the felicity he once knew; then, in the second half, he muses on the fragility and the mutability of the human condition, rising to a superb climax in the ancient *Ubi Sunt* motif ("Where now is the warhorse? Where now the noble rider?") which is one of the supreme passages in Old English poetry.

In *The Seafarer,* the first two sections follow a pattern similar to that of *The Wanderer.* The speaker describes, in a passage of notable lyric power, the hardships, loneliness, and fascination of life at sea; he then goes on in the second, "elegiac" section to recall some of the comforts and glories of life on land which he has repudiated, and to meditate (with a strongly Christian emphasis) upon the transience of earthly joys. The third and final section of the poem consists of general moralizing, and is poetically much inferior to the rest. There are, nevertheless, several passages in *The Seafarer,* especially the vividly detailed and moving picture of winter storms at sea, that are unsurpassed in Anglo-Saxon lyric poetry.

Religious Poetry

In one way or another nearly all of the extant verse in Old English is "religious" to some extent; even *Beowulf* is suffused with Christian lessons and Biblical references. The reason is not far to seek. The church, after all, was the fountain of literacy and sole purveyor of what education there was during these centuries. Consequently, nearly everything that was recorded in writing (the prose translations of Christian texts by King Alfred are rare exceptions) was the work of clerics – priests or monks – who would be unlikely to go to the trouble and expense of preserving literary works with absolutely no religious content. No doubt the Christian elements in *Beowulf* were all that saved that masterwork from oblivion; and the same is true of most of the other heroic or lyric poems that have come down to us. There is, inevitably, a considerable body of Old English poems that is entirely religious in subject matter and purpose.

Most of the religious poems in Old English are, quite naturally, derivative – that is to say they are based on famous stories from the Bible or from Christian mythology, such as *Exodus, Andreas,* or *Judith;* a very few seem to be original, including one masterpiece, *The Dream of the Rood.* The surprising fact, however, is that virtually all of these religious poems are composed not in a special spiritual mode of their own but in the standard heroic style of Germanic alliterative verse. They too, like *Beowulf,* or *The Wanderer,* or *The Battle of Maldon,* were intended not for reading but for oral performance before listening audiences steeped in the conventions of traditional Germanic poetry.

The earliest extant religious poetry in Old English, after the immensely popular and venerated *Hymn* of Caedmon (658–80) consisted of Old Testament paraphrases: *Genesis, Exodus,* and *Daniel.* The first of these has survived in a single manuscript combining two originally separate works, *Genesis A* and *Genesis B.* The A version (c. 700) follows the Biblical story fairly closely, but within this account is interpolated *Genesis B,* by a different and later poet (c. 875). *Genesis B* is a remarkably spirited account of the fall of Satan who is depicted in hell exhorting comrades like a Germanic chieftain with his *comitatus* of warriors. *Exodus* (c. 700) is an equally vivid account of the career of Moses, presented also in heroic terms in the native style with striking originality. *Daniel* is a quite vigorous, though incomplete, rendering of the old story. All of these Old Testament poems seems to belong to the tradition of Caedmon, and are usually called "Caedmonian." On the whole, *Exodus* is the finest of them.

The work of Cynewulf, who flourished somewhere north of the Thames about 800, is considerably more learned and sophisticated than the Caedmonian poems. Nothing is known of him except his name, which he wove into the text, in runic letters, of the four religious pieces that are certainly his work. These are: *The Fates of the Apostles,* brief and rather routine accounts of the lives and deaths of the twelve; *The Ascension* (also called *Christ II*), which contains some brilliant images; *Juliana,* a lively life of a Roman saint and martyr; and *Elene,* another Roman saint's life that is artistically the most exciting of the four. Elene (St. Helena) retrieves the true Cross from Jerusalem against impossible odds; she is presented by Cynewulf in traditional heroic style, with passages of real poetic power.

Finally, there is a group of half a dozen significant religious poems, dating roughly from 800 to 850, written in a style similar to that of Cynewulf though probably not by him. *Guthlac A* and *B* are two separate works celebrating the life of a native English saint, and both are fairly effective. *Christ I* is a group of lyrics or hymns glorifying the Advent, and including a remarkable dialogue between Joseph and Mary which may represent the earliest beginnings of the liturgical drama in England, a seed that bore fruit centuries later in the miracle plays of the fourteenth century. *Christ III* is a strongly imaginative account of the Last Judgment. *Andreas,* a vigorous narrative poem about the daring exploit of St. Andrew in rescuing St. Matthew from the clutches of the cannibal Mermedonians, is squarely in the tradition of Germanic heroic poetry, very similar in style to *Beowulf.* There is, even in this didactic Christian poem, the whole atmosphere of the ancient heroic (and heathen) mode – a dreadful storm at sea, a courageous leader, ring-giving, beer-drinking, desperate battles. The fragmentary *Judith,* based on the slaying of the Assyrian general Holofernes by the Old Testament heroine Judith, is likewise grim, forceful, and thoroughly Germanic.

By far the greatest of these Cynewulfian religious poems of the ninth century, however, is *The Dream of the Rood.* This astonishing work is presented as a dream-vision, the first in English poetry, in which the dreamer beholds a ceremonial cross (rood) that bleeds, and then speaks, recounting its life history from its beginnings in the forest to the time of the Crucifixion when it supported the body of Christ. Jesus is portrayed not as a victim of oppression but as a heroic leader of his people (again in the Germanic tradition), who achieved his final victory in this way. There are unforgettable moments in this poem, including the superb passage depicting the darkening of the skies at the beginning of the Crucifixion, building to a starkly dramatic climax in the simple statement "Christ waes on rode" (Christ was on the Cross). *The Dream of the Rood* is unique in Anglo-Saxon poetry in that it seems to be wholly original. In its profound emotion and poetic artistry it is unequalled in English religious poetry until the age of Chaucer five hundred years later.

The Norman Conquest

The natural development of Old English literary culture was brought to an abrupt halt by the Norman Conquest of 1066. This traumatic event wiped out the Anglo-Saxon monarchy and aristocracy and brought in a foreign, French-speaking ruling class in both state and church, as well as a new feudal system of land tenure. Though the Normans were never more than a small minority of the population (perhaps 10 percent), they succeeded under William the Conqueror in establishing complete and lasting control over the nation.

For literature the results were far reaching. At one stroke the old sources of support and patronage for writing in English – the church and royal courts – were destroyed. English was supplanted by French as the language of government, law, and literature; Latin, of course, continued as the language of learning; but English survived only as the spoken tongue of the mass of people. Except in a few isolated monasteries, English ceased to exist as a written language for nearly a century and a half. The varied and vital literary culture of the Anglo-Saxons which had produced, among other things, such sophisticated poetic masterpieces as *Beowulf*, *The Wanderer*, and *The Dream of the Rood* had come to an end.

MIDDLE ENGLISH LITERATURE

When English finally re-emerged as a written language around 1200, it had changed drastically in a number of ways. For several generations after the Conquest it had been a wholly oral tongue, and, in the absence of any literary standard, a fluid one subject to change. The elaborate inflections (case endings) of Old English had been largely slurred away, and the complicated verbal system greatly simplified. At the same time, the vocabulary had been enormously enriched by thousands of French words brought in by the Normans. During the entire Middle English phase of the history of the language (c. 1100–1485) something close to 10,000 words of French origin were absorbed and assimilated into English, virtually doubling its vocabulary. Whereas Old English seems to have been developing in its later phases something like a national literary standard superceding the local dialects, Middle English literature was composed for centuries in five distinct dialects (Northern, West Midland, East Midland, Southern, and Kentish); and it was not until the end of the era, about 1500, that East Midland – the language of London and Chaucer – finally prevailed as a literary standard for the whole country.

Our knowledge of Middle English literature is fragmentary since a great deal of it has been lost, but the writings that have survived run to hundreds of volumes in bulk and are incomparably more copious than the few precious remnants of Old English. Much of it is in prose, but, as in Old English times, the prose writings tend to be purely utilitarian or didactic in nature, and with few exceptions, notably the works of Sir Thomas Malory, they are of little value as literature. Again, as in the Old English era, education and literature continued to be dominated largely by the church. In theory at least, literature and the other arts existed for the sole purpose of buttressing religion and social morality, or, as Chaucer put it in his "Retractions" at the end of *The Canterbury Tales*, "all that is written is written for our doctrine [teaching]." In spite of this, however, several strongly secular genres emerged in the Middle English period, including romance, ballad, and fabliau, intended primarily for entertainment. During these centuries education and literacy developed steadily but very slowly; the literacy rate rose perhaps to ten percent by the age of Chaucer. The mass of the people and even some of the ruling class remained illiterate, and as a consequence poetry continued to be composed primarily for oral presentation and many of the oral traditions of Old English verse persisted for centuries. Dramatic changes in poetic form took place, however, with the importation from France of rhyme to replace alliteration as a primary technique, as well as elaborate new patterns of rhythm and stanza. Rhyme, of course, is (like alliteration) an aid to memory in recitation; and the older device of alliteration did not die out altogether but co-existed with rhyme for hundreds of years, especially in the north and the

West Midlands. Altogether, Middle English literature is naturally far richer and more varied than Old English, with several new genres emerging.

Romances

The romance was easily the most popular form of aristocratic secular literature of the late Middle Ages in England and in Western Europe generally. Comparable in many ways to the twentieth-century novel, in its breadth of appeal and variety of form, the romance is equally difficult to define and far more difficult for modern readers to appreciate. It may be long or short, in verse or prose, with or without love interest; but the romance is always a story of *adventure* involving famous kings, or knights, or distressed ladies, and governed by an elaborate code of literary conventions. Of the dozens of romances surviving in Middle English only three or four − by the Gawain Poet, Chaucer, and Malory − have established themselves through the sheer power of their art as permanent classics in our literature. Perhaps another three or four can still be read with some interest and pleasure, but a large majority of the romances seem boring and pointless to modern readers. The reason is that most romances, like most novels, were a kind of escapist literature, requiring little effort on the part of the reader, and therefore hugely popular. In the unheroic work-a-day lives of medieval people, full of dull routine and physical discomfort, the romance provided an escape into a dazzling dream world of ideal heroism, impossible virtue, and luxurious living.

The romance appears first in France in the twelfth century, evolving seemingly out of the earlier epic form called the *chanson de geste,* the most famous example of which is the *Chanson de Roland* (c. 1100). To the battle scenes and heroic exploits that were the exclusive subject matter of the *chanson de geste,* however, a large new dimension − the elaborate French code of courtly behavior and of love − was added by the great French poet Chrétien de Troyes, who wrote in the period from about 1160 to 1190. In so doing, Chrétien more or less created the new genre of the romance. But for his subject matter Chrétien went not to French heroes but to the freshly emerging legends of Celtic British origins concerning King Arthur and his knights. The fountainhead of these Arthurian stories had appeared a generation earlier in the Latin chronicle *History of the Kings of Britain* (1137) by an Englishman, Geoffrey of Monmouth, a work based partly on Welsh oral traditions but copiously amplified by the pure invention of the author. Geoffrey's *History* was promptly translated into Norman French by Wace, whose *Roman de Brut* (1155) contains important additions to the story, including the whole business of the round table. Wace's version, in turn, was re-created in English about 1200 by Layamon in *The Brut,* a largely expanded patriotic epic poem (more than twice as long as Wace's), which combines the traditional alliteration carried over from the Old English style with the new device of rhyme. At any rate, Chrétien de Troyes seized upon this exciting Arthurian material as he found it in Geoffrey or Wace or other French translations and developed it further in five highly sophisticated verse romances. The success of the new form was immediate, and it promptly spread through Western Europe.

The romance reached England in the thirteenth century. The earliest surviving specimens in our language, *King Horn* and *Havelok,* seem to date from about 1250, and are far less sophisticated than the brilliant prototypes of Chrétien. *Havelok,* nevertheless, with its home-bred English characters and scenes, has some real charm and interest. But the next century, the fourteenth, is the golden age of the romance in England, when literally dozens of them were composed. Most of them, of course, are mediocre or uninspired as works of art, including such popular titles as *Guy of Warwick* and *Bevis of Hampton* (both c. 1300), the English *Song of Roland* (c. 1325), and *Sir Ferumbras* (c. 1400). The century did produce, however, five or six romances of genuine distinction. Of these the earliest is *Sir Orfeo* (c. 1320), a so-called "Breton Lay," that is, a short verse romance dealing with Breton or at least Celtic characters. (Chaucer's *Franklin's Tale* is the finest of the type in English.) *Sir Orfeo* is a Celticized rendering of the ancient Greek myth of Orpheus and Eurydice, but with a happy ending. It is essentially a fairy story − lively, witty, and delightful. More impressive is the

Alliterative Morte Arthur (c. 1360), one of the best renderings of the Arthurian story in Middle English, with strong characterization, some brilliant scenes, and vigorous narrative skill throughout. Also classifiable as romance is the memorable poem in Middle Scots called *The Bruce* (1376) by John Barbour, a powerfully romanticized account of the exploits of Robert Bruce, King of Scots, in securing the independence of Scotland against the English incursions under Edward II. Motivated by patriotism, Barbour's poem is often dramatic and enthralling, with some truly eloquent passages.

We come, next, to the greatest of all verse romances in our language – those of the Gawain Poet and Chaucer. *Sir Gawain and the Green Knight* was written in the northwest Midland area of England by an unknown poet about 1375. In the superb artistry of its narrative technique, in its fusion of rollicking humor and moral seriousness, and in sheer poetic expressiveness, *Sir Gawain* remains one of finest things of its kind in any literature. It is the story of the testing of a good man's honor in love and fortitude in the face of deadly combat; there is tremendous suspense as Gawain is humbled at the end by his human frailty while maintaining the essential nobility of his character. The more often one reads *Sir Gawain and the Green Knight* the richer and more dazzling it seems – which is a sure indication of great art. Chaucer's *Knight's Tale* (c. 1380) is not quite so good, but it is nevertheless a work of high distinction. In the conventional heroics of love and war, brilliantly described with touches of humor, are interlarded passages of philosophical commentary that are very unusual in the romance as a genre. Yet in *Troilus and Criseyde* (1385) Chaucer went a great deal farther in extending the dimensions of romance. The most astonishing quality of this astonishing poem is the fullness and the psychological depth of characterization. We have Troilus, the noble idealist, obsessed by his love for Criseyde; Pandarus, the pragmatic go-between, cynical, witty, garrulous, amusingly cunning in the ways of the world; Criseyde, the canny, brilliant heroine, and ambivalent woman of infinite charm and fascination – all struggling against but drifting toward their tragic destiny. Seldom have the agonies and joys of sexual love been treated with such profound and convincing insight. *Troilus and Criseyde,* indeed, so far transcends its genre that some critics have been reluctant to label it as a romance at all, though it has all the trappings of the form. However one characterizes it, Chaucer's *Troilus* is one of the supreme long poems in English literature, one of the great love stories. It is also, considered as a single, perfectly wrought work (not counting *The Canterbury Tales* as such), the greatest artistic achievement in Middle English.

After reaching its apex in *Sir Gawain* and *Troilus,* the romance declined steadily in the course of the fifteenth century. The age of chivalry itself was by then pretty much a thing of the past; the feudal system introduced by William the Conqueror was slowly disintegrating; and a new, prosperous middle class with different literary interests was coming to the fore. The romance, then, was dying a natural death along with the aristocratic feudal culture which had given birth to it. In the light of these historical trends, it is rather surprising to find a sudden and final re-surgence of the genre at the very end of the Middle English era in the works of Sir Thomas Malory. Surprising, too, is the fact that, whereas most of the English romances are in verse, Malory chose to write in prose. A vast and growing amount of prose writing was produced in Middle English, but most of it, including that of Chaucer, is loose in structure or awkward seeming, vaguely dissatisfying, at least to modern readers. Malory's is the first truly artistic prose style in the language, and for that reason he is also, in a real sense, the father of English prose fiction. His work has been traditionally but erroneously called the *Morte Darthur* (a title that properly belongs only to the final section), and seems to have been intended as a series of eight separate romances rather than a single continuing story. Derived primarily from the huge accumulation of Arthurian romances in French, but including also some English sources (notably the *Alliterative Morte Arthur*), Malory's book is a superb reworking of the most exciting episodes and characters from the sprawling mass of legends about Arthur and his knights. Though Malory is looking back to the "good old days" of knight-errantry with nostalgia, his remarkable economy of expression and skillful management of great scenes make his work always entertaining, always readable, occasionally quite moving (as in the famous closing description of the death of Arthur).

Altogether, Malory's lively and masterly work makes a fitting finale to the history of the romance in Middle English.

Ballads

At the opposite end of the social scale from the aristocratic romance we have the ballad, a form of oral folk literature. Most of the folk or "popular" ballads that have come down to us seem to date from the late Middle Ages – thirteenth, fourteenth, and fifteenth centuries – though some are as late as the seventeenth. Ballads are always short narratives in verse made to be sung to traditional tunes. They usually deal with sensational events – tragic love, sexual scandal, suicide, abduction, treachery, murder, magic, mayhem – and most were probably composed to commemorate actual local incidents as heightened by the folk imagination. The authors, of course, are anonymous, and of the more than 300 extant ballads only a handful can be connected with known historical occurences. "Sir Patrick Spens" for example, may possibly record a shipwreck which took place in 1290, but the subjects of most ballads are unknown to history.

Today it is generally believed that the ballads are the work of gifted individuals who functioned in their local communities both as skilled composers in a traditional style and meter and as singers of their own work and that of others. They were analagous to the Old English scops, though in a somewhat humbler professional and social status. Composed orally by specialists of this kind, the ballads were passed on orally from generation to generation. No doubt thousands of ballads were created, but only the best – those that caught the popular imagination by their dramatic power and artistry – persisted through the centuries. Most of the great ballads remained unrecorded in writing until the eighteenth century when educated people became interested in "primitive" art of various kinds. The pioneer ballad-hunters of the eighteenth century – men like Thomas Percy, David Herd, and Walter Scott – often wrote down the texts as they heard them straight from the lips of local singers. As a consequence, though the ballads are mainly medieval in origin, the language in which they have been preserved is relatively modern. Moreover, the language is most often Scots rather than standard English, and the reason for this is clear. The ballad as an oral form can flourish only in communities that are predominately illiterate. As soon as mass education moves in the ballad dies and is replaced by written forms of literature. By the time the British ballads were finally recorded, the genre had died out as a living art form in most of England and in the more cultivated parts of Scotland; but it was still thriving in two areas, both cultural backwaters that were as yet relatively untouched by modern civilization. These were the hilly and isolated Border country of Southern Scotland and the hill country of Aberdeenshire in the northeast. And it was to these two pockets of oral culture in Scotland that the eighteenth-century ballad enthusiasts had to go to find their material.

The oral nature of the folk ballad accounts for several of its special characteristics and also for much of the fascination and distinctive charm it holds for modern readers. Since most ballads circulated in oral transmission for hundreds of years before they were written down, they existed in a kind of fluid form subject to change and revision in details and language as they moved from one generation or geographical area to another. As a result, virtually all of the ballads have come down to us in multiple versions, sometimes in *dozens* of versions. For the same reason, the ballad is strangely impersonal in style: whatever feeling it may once have had of the personality of the original author has long since been filtered out in the process of oral transmission. The frequent use of refrains (sometimes meaningless) and of other kinds of repetition as aids to memory is obviously a device to make things easier both for the performer and for the listeners. Furthermore, the oral situation is reflected in the fact that the ballads clearly employ certain traditional patterns – in verse form, structure, subject matter, and diction – all of which must have been intimately familiar to medieval audiences.

Of these stereotyped patterns the most obvious is the so-called "Ballad Stanza" used in the majority of the extant pieces. It is a four-lined stanza of alternating tetrameters and trimeters, rhymed A B C B, as in "The Wife of Usher's Well":

> There lived a wife at Usher's Well
> And a wealthy wife was she;
> She had three stout and stalwart sons
> And sent them o'er the sea.

In narrative structure the typical method is to plunge immediately into the dramatic crisis of the situation, without preliminaries, and then to fill in the needed background information gradually or indirectly. Among the great ballads that follow this traditional pattern are "Bonny Barbara Allan," "Lord Randall," "Edward," and "The Twa Corbies." In the treatment of their subject matter the ballad makers drew freely upon a vast store of folklore motifs that were international in circulation and must have been well known to British audiences. Many British ballads have their counterparts in Continental balladry (especially Scandinavian) for this reason. Ballads of the supernatural kind, in particular, are apt to use this common fund of folklore. No doubt even ballads based on actual local events (and most probably were) were often adapted to fit into some traditional motif or other. In diction, too, the ballads make extensive use of traditional formulas, though they tend to be simpler and more straightforward than the oral formulas of Old English poetry. One has only to read fifteen or twenty ballads to become aware of phrases that recur. Some of these verbal stereotypes are particularly distinctive, such as "he tirled at the pin" (knocked at the door), or "he took out his wee penknife" (a favorite weapon of ballad heroes and villains alike).

The finest of the folk ballads are not really "primitive" at all; they are great works of art by unknown masters working within a rich and fairly complex oral tradition. Indeed, among the short poems in all of English literature it would be hard to find anything to beat the eerie sepulchral tone of "The Twa Corbies" or the smashing dramatic force of "Edward." In narrative technique, to take a single example, "Edward" is superb. This question-and-answer ballad opens with Edward stricken with remorse, his sword dripping blood. For three stanzas he evades his mother's questions before finally confessing that he has slain his father. This introduction serves to build suspense, while at the same time it rings true psychologically – Edward needs time to bring himself to face the full horror of what he has done. In the questions and answers that follow more of the background is slowly revealed or hinted at, but the poet holds back until the very last line of the ballad his revelation of the ghastly fact that Edward's greedy and vicious mother has instigated the crime:

> "And what wul ye'leave to your ain mither dear,
>   Edward, Edward?
> And what wul ye leave to your ain mither dear,
>   My dear son, now tell me, O?"
> "The curse of hell frae me sal ye bear,
>   Mither, mither,
> The curse of hell frae me sal ye bear,
>   Sic such counseils ye gave to me, O."

There are not many effects as breathtaking as this in the English and Scottish ballads, but dozens of them are beautifully wrought, with a strange stark power that is entrancing.

Lyrics

Unlike the ballad, which was purely oral, the Middle English lyric was a form of written literature, though these poems were often performed as songs or dances with musical accompaniment. Hundreds of lyrics, the majority anonymous, have survived in English from these centuries, and they show an extraordinary variety of subject matter and styles. They range, indeed, from the solemnly religious to the downright bawdy, from the highly sophisticated to the naively simple. This fact suggests that the audiences for late medieval lyric poetry must have been equally varied, including the entire gamut of social classes –

aristocracy and clergy, literate middle class, as well as the commonfolk. As might be expected, much of this poetry is religious in inspiration, but the line separating secular from sacred verse is often blurred, with sensuous images occurring in poems devoted to the Virgin Mary, for example, or religious symbols appearing in what seem to be secular love songs. Religion was then so integral a part of the daily lives of all people that the medieval mind saw no inconsistency in such practices, and they may be observed clearly enough in the lyrics of known poets. William Dunbar (c. 1460–c. 1522), for instance, who wrote "In secreit place this hynder nycht," a comically obscene love poem, was also the author of exalted religious lyrics such as his soaring celebration of the Resurrection, "Done is a battell on the dragon blak." The same kind of range and mixture of sacred and profane is readily evident in the lyrics of Chaucer, Henryson, and others.

Middle English lyrics contrast sharply with modern lyric poetry in that they lack the subjective personal quality we have come to expect in this genre. The medieval lyric depends heavily on fixed literary conventions: the more sophisticated courtly pieces are usually built upon elaborate patterns derived from Provençal, French, or medieval Latin poetic conventions; the stylistically simpler kinds of lyrics are founded upon native formulas of folk expression. As in the ballad there is seldom much sense of the individuality of the author. Yet within these stylized limitations the Middle English lyric at its best achieves freshness and vitality that are elusive but altogether delightful.

These fine qualities may easily be illustrated. Among the sacred lyrics of the simpler kind is the well known "I Sing of a Maiden" (thirteenth century), a charming and tender tribute to the Virgin. Here are the first two and final stanzas:

> I sing of a maiden
>   That is makelees* :   *matchless
> King of alle kinges
>   To her sone she chees*.   *chose
>
> He cam also stille
>   Ther* his moder was   *where
> As dewe in Aprille
>   That falleth on the gras.
>
> Moder and maiden
>   Was nevere noon but she:
> Wel may swich* a lady   *such
>   Godes moder be.

Among secular lyrics the same kind of simple, pithy, lilting quality may be enjoyed in dozens of pieces, including the famous "Sumer is icumen in" (fourteenth century) or in this tiny gem of a love poem of the same period:

> All night by the rose, rose,
>   All night by the rose I lay;
> Darf ich* nought the rose stele,   *dared I
>   And yet ich bar* the flour away.   *bore

Perhaps half of the extant lyrics in Middle English share the concise, direct, folksy style just illustrated. The remainder are far more complex, more "literary" in manner, and generally based on patterns derived from French or Latin. In this large category belong the fine courtly lyrics of Chaucer such as "Gentilesse," "Truth," and "To Rosemounde"; the powerful short poems of Robert Henryson, including his wholly delightful pastoral called "Robene and Makyne"; many pieces by Dunbar and by other known poets; as well as an important body of anonymous works. Into this last group fall many elaborate lyrics, such as

"The Thrush and the Nightingale" (thirteenth century), an amusing debate between two birds on the frailties and merits of women, and the highly entertaining dialogue between two lovers called "The Nut-Brown Maid" (fifteenth century). Again, the most surprising quality of the Middle English lyric, whether religious or secular, simple or sophisticated, is the extent to which strong emotional effects are attained while working within the strict confines of impersonal comventional formulas. The result, at least in the finer specimens, is a very special kind of charm, a delightful art that is difficult to define but wholly distinctive and recognizable.

Religious and Didactic Literature

The majority of writings in Middle English, as in all periods, is utilitarian in nature. But in contrast to modern times there was relatively little emphasis upon information for its own sake; instead, the main thrust of literature in these centuries is in the direction of religious and moral instruction or inspiration. As a result, there are countless manuals of devotional and ethical instruction, bushels of saints' lives, sermons, mystical visions, all kinds of religious and moral allegories, didactic fables, exempla (tales teaching moral lessons), and so forth. As might be expected, most of the hundreds of volumes of these in Middle English are pedestrian in style, clumsy in structure; only a very small proportion of this vast body rises to the level of literary art. This is especially true of the work in prose, to which we may turn briefly.

Middle English prose before Sir Thomas Malory is generally negligible as literature, but there are a few exceptional pieces. The earliest of these is *The Ancrene Riwle* (c. 1200), a book of advice written by an unknown priest for three young ladies who were about to become religious hermits (anchoresses). Despite its rather forbidding purpose, the "Rule for Anchoresses" remains readable and entertaining, thanks to many passages of wise and gentle humor, homely pictures of everyday life, and, occasionally, strokes of brilliant imagination. Then, in the early fourteenth century we have the voluminous prose work of the mystic Richard Rolle, best read in excerpts, who at times rises to moments of passionate emotional power that are extraordinarily moving. The age of Chaucer in the last half of the fourteenth century also produced a few notable achievements in prose, including the "Wyclif" Bible, the first complete translation of the Bible into English. Inspired by the great religious reformer John Wyclif, but mostly the work of his gifted disciples (especially John Purvey), the Wyclif Bible is a strong and often eloquent rendering of the Latin Vulgate; it remained a potent stylistic influence upon much later translations, including those of Tyndale and Coverdale in the sixteenth century and the King James Bible in the seventeenth. To the same period belongs the amusing *Travels of Sir John Mandeville,* first written in French, then translated into English, a sprightly travel book, partly fictitious but always entertaining, with some genuine narrative skill. Finally, there are the prose works of Chaucer himself, especially the *Tale of Melibee* and the *Parson's Tale,* which, though unexciting for modern readers on the whole, have some interesting and pleasurable passages.

The achievement of Middle English religious and didactic literature is far more substantial in verse than in prose. The earliest surviving piece of real excellence is the debate in verse between two birds, *The Owl and the Nightingale* (c. 1200), by an unknown author. The poem is in rhymed couplets, but with a considerable overlay of alliteration (evidence of the continuing vitality of Old English methods). The argument has been variously interpreted, usually as an allegorical presentation of the philosophical ascetic ideal (owl) versus the active sensual life (nightingale) with the poet in the middle. It may even be a burlesque of the debate itself as a popular teaching device. Whatever its purpose, *The Owl and the Nightingale* is a very skillful and spirited poem, often extremely diverting – a small masterpiece of delightful "instruction." Another early example of wit and wisdom is *The Land of Cockayne* (c. 1275), though it is harsher in its implications, being a cutting satire on the corruption of the monastic orders. "The land of Cockayne" is a dreamland of milk and honey where fat Cistercian monks wallow in luxury and sex while the rest of the world must work for a living. The conception is highly imaginative, the style lively and amusing. Robert Mannyng's *Handlyng Synne* (1303) also deserves mention as a didactic work of some literary merit. This very long poem, a "manual" or catalogue of sins, could have been extremely dull, but is redeemed by dozens of entertaining anecdotes used to illustrate various points.

The late fourteenth century is the golden age of religious and didactic verse, as it is of imaginative literature in general. The greatest of all Middle English poets – the Gawain Poet, Langland, and, above all, Chaucer – belong to this period, to the same generation in fact, and all worked mightily in religio-didactic genres. The three religious poems attributed to the Gawain Poet, and almost certainly by him, are *Patience, Cleanness*, and *Pearl*. The first two are powerful re-creations of Old Testament stories – those of Jonah, the Flood, Sodom, and Belshazzar's Feast – enriched with fine dramatic effects, humor, pathos, and excellent imagery. These poems, along with the rest of the works of the Gawain Poet, and of Langland, are composed in the traditional alliterative style inherited from Old English, and thus are part of the fourteenth-century "Alliterative Revival" in the west and north-west of England. More dazzling than *Patience* and *Cleanness,* however, is *Pearl,* which combines alliteration with a complex pattern of 101 stanzas of twelve lines each, connected by interlocking rhymes. As a technical *tour de force* the poem is mind-boggling; as a movingly imaginative dream-vision of spiritual loss and redemption *Pearl* is the greatest religious poem in English since *The Dream of the Rood* and one of the supreme achievements of its kind in all of literature.

Very different is the vast, rambling poem of William Langland which is now usually called *Piers Plowman.* A cleric, probably from Shropshire who lived mostly in London, Langland devoted his entire lifetime to this huge work which has come down to us in three versions (A, B, and C), dating from the 1360's into the 1390's. The poem is both a satire on the corruption and mercenary hypocrisy of his society as Langland saw it, and at the same time, an absorbing account of the poet's search for a new way to spiritual salvation – a simple, honest Christian way through love, as exemplified in the vision by the Christ-like figure of the humble peasant Piers. What saves this ambitious work from dullness is Langland's sheer human vitality, his zest for living in this world, combined with his ability to *visualize* experience, to transform theological and moral concepts into concrete physical images of human life, and vice versa. These qualities raise a poem that is often loosely, even confusingly, put together to the level of great art; they make it compellingly interesting, and one of the most powerful religious and social documents of the Middle Ages.

With Geoffrey Chaucer, as so often with the greatest writers, the lines of distinction between conventional literary genres are frequently blurred or transcended, as we have already noted in connection with *Troilus and Criseyde.* Though Chaucer seems "modern" in some ways (in his intense interest in probing human psychology, for example), in most respects he was solidly medieval in his aims and attitudes. Consequently, much of his work tends to be religio-didactic in nature; yet relatively little of it is exclusively so. Apart from his prose writings, which are purely instructional, we have only three of *The Canterbury Tales* – the saints' lives told by the Man of Law, the Prioress, and the Second Nun – that fall strictly within the category. But how should we classify something like the *Nun's Priest's Tale* of Chauntecler and Pertelote? In form it is a beast fable which, by definition, teaches a lesson, or several lessons, in this case; but it is far more than that. It is also one of the most brilliantly entertaining verse narratives in literature, rich in subtle ironies, wise humor, outrageous burlesques. The *Nun's Priest's Tale,* in short, is mixed in its artistic purposes, and this is true of most of Chaucer's didactic verse. Of his earlier poems certainly *The House of Fame* (c. 1379) and *The Parlement of Foules* (c. 1380) fall into this hybrid class, as does *The Legend of Good Women* (c. 1386), and perhaps even the elegiac *Book of the Duchesse* (c. 1369). The *Canterbury Tales* themselves are full of this kind of "delightful instruction," most notably in the stories told by the Clerk, the Franklin, the Pardoner, the Monk, the Nun's Priest, the Canon's Yeoman, and the Manciple. Chaucer's range is enormous, his imagination multi-faceted. As a result, much of his work, especially his greatest work, cannot easily be labeled or pigeon-holed. He is interested in all aspects of human life and character, as well as in man's relationship to God. Hence, though most of his poetry has some religious or didactic dimension, it is seldom limited exclusively to such purposes; rather it extends to a rich complexity.

The unique power and greatness of Chaucer can readily be appreciated by contrasting his work with that of his contemporary and friend John Gower, "moral Gower" as Chaucer aptly called him. Gower's one large achievement in English verse, *Confessio Amantis* (Confessions of a Lover), has considerable merit. It is a vast collection of 133 tales used to illustrate various moral and ethical lessons, set within a fairly effective "framework" device. The narrative frame, however, is more or less static, lacking the fascinating interplay of characters that enlivens *The Canterbury Tales*. The stories themselves are explicitly didactic and generally well written in clear, flowing verse. The best of them are genuinely interesting, all are readable. Gower, is, in fact, a good poet, an able creative intelligence who has often been undervalued because he is overshadowed by Chaucer; but in the final analysis he simply does not have the elusive magic of genius, the subtle ambiguity, the irresistible imaginative force of his friend and master.

In religious and didactic verse, as in other kinds of poetry, the fifteenth century in England is a period of dismal decline, following the golden age of Chaucer. (I am excluding here the work of the Scottish poets which will be treated in a separate section.) This era produced nothing comparable to the splendors of the Gawain Poet, Langland, Chaucer himself, or even the solid talents of Gower. Part of the problem, no doubt, was that the immense reputation of Chaucer encouraged servile imitations; more important, no truly gifted poets appeared on the English scene for several generations. The chief English disciples of Chaucer, John Lydgate and Thomas Hoccleve, rarely rise above the level of mediocrity. During a long lifetime Lydgate produced an enormous amount of verse (over 145,000 lines), all doggedly moralistic – so much that a large part of it remains unprinted, understandably, after 500 years. Hoccleve, on the whole, is more interesting (which is not saying much) mainly by virtue of his modest stylistic skill and his frank personal revelations about his life and problems as a young man about London in the early 1400's. In general, the work of these men and of other nameless English poets of the fifteenth century has cultural or historical interest but little literary value.

Fabliaux

Like the romance, the fabliau is a French literary invention of the late Middle Ages. It may be defined as a humorous short story in verse, dealing with middle or lower class characters, and involving some kind of trickery or practical joke. The fabliau was extremely popular in France, whence it spread to other countries, but it never became a major genre in Britain (only about a dozen English and Scottish specimens have survived). In the typical French fabliau the emphasis is upon the sequence of comic events, upon the ingenuity of the trick; characterization and setting are minimal, and the characters are usually no more than types – the scheming wife, clever lover, foolish husband, duped merchant, and so forth. This pattern is apparent in the anonymous British examples, ranging from the early *Dame Sirith* (c. 1300) to the late *Freiris of Berwick* (c. 1500), as it is also in Chaucer's *Shipman's Tale*.

The supreme accomplishment in the fabliau in our language, or in any language, is the work of Chaucer in the tales of the Miller, Reeve, and Merchant in the Canterbury series. In these great tales – and to a lesser extent in those of the Friar, Summoner, and Manciple – Chaucer once again transforms and transcends the genre in which he is working. He does this by combining the usual comic plot with vastly enriched characterization, setting, and emotional atmosphere, so that the hilarious climax seems to arise inevitably out of the characters of the chief personages in each story; at the same time the tale reflects the peculiar traits of its pilgrim teller. The result is a rich, complex, human comedy, contrived yet convincing, making these tales among the funniest in our language. The fabliau is, of course, the most purely secular (almost frivolous) genre in Middle English; but in the hands of Chaucer at his superb best it reaches the level of high art.

Middle Scots Poetry

The finest British poetry of the fifteenth century was written in Scotland, but this remains unreflected in the practice of literary historians and critics. In a very recent work, for example, one critic readily admits the striking superiority of the Scots poets of this century, but then goes on to devote to them only about one third of the space given to the English poets of the same period. Dreary Lydgate regularly gets more attention than sparkling Henryson. Whatever the reasons, there is no excuse for this absurd imbalance.

Scottish literature developed relatively late, not emerging in any significant way until the fourteenth century. Its chief monument in the early phase is Barbour's fine romance of *Bruce* (1376) written, like all subsequent Scottish literature for the next two hundred years, in the language called Middle Scots. Middle Scots is very closely related to Middle English (and scarcely more difficult for modern readers) since it was an independent development from the northern dialect of Old English. The extant prose writing in Middle Scots is historical or utilitarian and is of little value as literature. But the poetry is a different story. In this medium we have a golden age of brilliant and sophisticated work in Middle Scots, extending from about 1420 to 1520, an age that produced at least six known poets of real distinction – King James I, Sir Richard Holland, Blind Hary, Robert Henryson, William Dunbar, and Gavin Douglas – as well as a host of talented anonymous authors. During this period the Scottish court (especially during the reigns of James I, James IV, and James V) became one of the most dynamic cultural centers in Europe, far surpassing, in poetic achievement at least, what was going on in England. This poetry may be divided into three broad classifications. First, there is the aristocratic "courtly" poetry in Middle Scots which includes all of the general European genres shared by England – romance, love allegory, dream-vision, religio-didactic works in the high style. At the other end of the scale there is a flourishing tradition of folk poetry, mostly ballads and folk songs, already discussed here. Finally, there is a large and important category, especially prominent in Scotland, that may be termed art poetry on folk themes.

In the courtly category obviously belongs the fine long poem by King James I of Scotland called *The Kingis Quair* (King's Book). This love allegory, presumably a re-creation of James's actual courting and winning of his English wife, Lady Jane Beaufort, is written in Chaucer's seven-line "rime royal" stanza. Though clearly influenced by Chaucer, the poem has a life of its own, a personal charm and vitality that are exceptional in this conventional genre. Very different are the two other poems attributed (uncertainly) to James I, *Peblis to the Play* and *Christis Kirk on the Green.* These delightful pieces are comic satires on the antics of groups of bungling peasants on festive occasions, full of drunkenness, horseplay, and mild bawdry, as seen from the point of view of an amused and superior spectator. They became the prototypes of a distinctively Scottish poetic genre, the *"Christis Kirk* tradition," which flourished in Scotland for centuries, culminating in some of the poems of Robert Burns (e.g., *The Holy Fair* and *The Jolly Beggars*) nearly 400 years later. Written in a special ten-line stanza, combining a difficult rhyme scheme with alliteration, *Peblis* and *Christis Kirk* are brilliantly entertaining specimens of art poetry on folk themes.

In the middle decades of the fifteenth century we have the work of two able poets or "makaris" (makers), to use the Scots term, Sir Richard Holland and Blind Hary. Holland's *Buke of the Howlat* (owl) is a lengthy political allegory, presenting a vivid dream of a reformed and rejuvenated Europe in place of current corruptions and contentiousness. Hary's *Wallace* is an epic account of the Scottish hero, embellished with fictional episodes, and even more fiercely patriotic than Barbour's *Bruce.* Wallace is conceived as a tragic hero in scenes that are intensely visual. The poem is relatively crude in style, but has remarkable emotional force.

Toward the end of the century Middle Scots poetry reached its peak in the work of Henryson, Dunbar, and Douglas, the three greatest British poets of their age. For a long time Robert Henryson was remembered only as the author of *The Testament of Cresseid,* but more recently the full range of his accomplishment has come to be recognized. His longest and in some ways greatest work is the collection of thirteen *Moral Fables* he adapted from Aesop. In each of these Henryson takes the bare bones of the fable as inherited from Aesop and expands it with the addition of rich characterization, Scottish milieu, and a variety of commentary on contemporary issues – social, religious, political, and moral. In other words, he totally re-creates the fable as Chaucer had done in *The Nun's Priest's Tale*, but he does it in his own highly original style, with his own special brand of wry Scots humor. *The Testament of Cresseid*, of course, suffers by contrast to the far longer and more complex masterpiece of Chaucer, to which it is a sort of sequel; but the *Testament* has a tight narrative structure and grim, Henrysonian ironies that make it, despite its narrow scope, a great and unforgettable poem in its own right. Among Henryson's several shorter poems, his irresistible pastoral "Robene and Makyne" stands out. Beginning readers of Middle Scots should start with this perfectly crafted little poem. In it the girl Makyne begs the shepherd Robene to make love to her; he rejects her cruelly, but on his way home has a change of heart and rushes back – too late. Makyne triumphantly informs him that "The man that will nocht whan he may/Sal have nocht whan he wald [would]." Had Henryson written nothing else, he would have deserved immortality for this wonderfully funny jewel of a poem.

William Dunbar, born a generation later than Henryson, is a different kind of poet. Whereas Henryson has a serene view of life with a quiet insinuative humor, Dunbar is an emotional extremist, a virtuoso who does nothing by halves. When he writes about his fear of death (as in the great "Lament for the Makaris") he is terrifying; when he wishes to be obscenely funny (as in "In secreit place this hinder nycht" or in his anti-feminist satire "The Treatis of the Twa Maryit Wemen and the Wedo") he is very obscene and very funny; when he is in a religious mood (as in the poems on the Resurrection or on the Virgin) his verse is soaring and exalted. Dunbar's emotional range is extraordinary; his technical brilliance in a wide variety of verse forms is dazzling. Of the three great Scots makers, Henryson is the most endearing writer, but Dunbar is the most exciting. Probably his finest single work is the devastating "Treatis" in which the satire is double-edged. The two married women and the widow are, of course, appalling creatures (as in most anti-feminist satire), morally depraved, sexually insatiable, totally unscrupulous; but they are also *victims* of a pernicious socio-economic system, a system of marriage laws and attitudes that makes them what they are. Dunbar sees, and makes us see, both sides of the coin. Here, as elsewhere, his imaginative power is breath-taking.

Gavin Douglas, a few years younger than his contemporary Dunbar, is the last of the great poets in Middle Scots. His fame rests upon the *Eneados*, his translation of Virgil's *Aeneid*, including thirteen wholly original "prologues" for the various books. Both the translation itself and the prologues are poetic achievements of high excellence. Douglas's translation is "free," robust, and eloquent, combining the precision of imported (Scoticized) Latinate vocabulary with the pithiness of vernacular Scots to capture the spirit and flavor of the great Roman epic – so good, in fact, that it remains after nearly five hundred years as one of the finest translations of Virgil in British literature. The prologues, too, covering a broad gamut of subjects, are intensely interesting and beautifully written.

The Drama

Among the new genres that emerged in the Middle English period (romance, ballad, fabliau, etc.) the last to arrive on the scene was the secularized drama. It did not appear in full-blown form until the fourteenth century, although the liturgical drama out of which it evolved was hundreds of years older. The great tradition of ancient Greek and Roman drama had died out with the collapse of the Roman Empire about 500, and for close to five centuries thereafter no organized drama, as far as we know, existed in Western Europe. Medieval drama, therefore, was a fresh beginning, totally independent of the work of the ancients which had been almost wholly lost and forgotten. Coincidentally, like the Greek drama the medieval seems to have developed out of religious rites.

In Western Europe generally, beginning about the year 900, some tentative dramatic elements began to be introduced in churches in liturgical ceremonies connected with the festival of Easter. Short dialogues (or "tropes") were acted out by clerics in an attempt to make the Bible story more meaningful to illiterate congregations. So successful and popular were these experiments that they were gradually expanded over a long period of time, and a tradition of short religious plays performed in the churches slowly developed. At first the religious plays were in Latin, but at some point they shifted to the vernacular tongues; at first they were limited to Easter scenes, but then spread to include Christmas and other important dates in the religious calendar. Not much is known about this early liturgical drama, but it is certain that it existed and that in England, probably in the early fourteenth century, the plays were moved out of the churches and into the marketplaces where they were taken over by the guilds of tradesmen in various towns.

No one really knows why this change took place. It has often been supposed that the plays themselves had become so secularized that the Church could no longer countenance them, but it seems more likely that they were moved outdoors simply because they had become too elaborate in staging and in props or too popular to be easily accommodated in the church buildings. At any rate, the religious plays were taken over by the guilds in England, each guild assuming responsibility for a single play. The plays were grouped together in great "cycles" covering important Biblical episodes from the Old and New Testaments in chronological order from the Creation to the Last Judgment. Instead of being performed periodically throughout the year as they had been in the churches, the plays were now (probably because of outdoor weather conditions) presented all at once in the spring around Corpus Christi Day as a kind of annual dramatic festival lasting two or three days.

A cycle of "miracle plays," as they are now generally called (though the term "mystery play" is sometimes also used), would normally begin with one or more Creation plays, followed by a Cain and Abel play, Noah, Abraham and Isaac, and so on through the Old Testament and into the New, starting with Nativity plays and others dramatizing episodes in the life of Jesus, leading to a Crucifixion play, then the Resurrection, and finally the Last Judgment or Doomsday play. Only four such cycles have survived more or less complete in Middle English, those of Chester (twenty-five plays), York (forty-eight plays), Wakefield (thirty-two plays), and, probably, Lincoln (forty-two plays), plus fragments of two or three others; but many other English towns, including London, must have had their miracle plays as well. Some of the Wakefield plays are very closely related verbally to their counterparts in the York cycle, suggesting that the Wakefield guilds "borrowed" some scripts from the neighboring town, or vice versa.

How were these miracle plays produced? Here again there are many uncertainties, but it seems clear from the sparse historical records that they were usually performed on horsedrawn wagons called "pageants" which could be moved from one town square or open space to another, or even from one town to another. The pageant wagons seemed to have varied in design: the simpler ones had one storey only; others had two (with the enclosed lower storey as a kind of dressing room); some had a balcony superstructure for the presentation of elevated characters such as God. The audience surrounded these movable stages on all four sides. There was no artificial barrier separating actors from audience as in most modern theatres; instead, the actors played directly to the audience, with evil characters making faces at the spectators, and (no doubt) frequent pauses for applause, laughter, and booing. It was a dynamic, often rambunctious, kind of theatre despite its basic religious motivations, and it established an acting tradition that persisted in the English theatre for hundreds of years − until the early nineteenth century, in fact. The acting itself was probably very good, semi-professional, as each guild put on the same play year after year, generation after generation, developing highly skilled actors for each part. Certainly by the end of the fourteenth century the miracle plays in England had become a flourishing national drama, immensely popular, vital, and democratic − a drama which provided a solid base for the flowering of the great Elizabethan theatre two hundred years later.

How do these miracle plays stand up as literature? At a first reading most of them seem less than exciting for modern students of drama, and for two very good reasons. Most importantly, these plays, like all drama, were intended not to be read in the silence of the study but to be *seen* and *heard* on a lively outdoor stage, performed by actors under the warm spring sunshine. Secondly, the simple and unquestioning religious faith that inspired them is largely a thing of the past. In the later phase of their evolution the miracle plays had, of course, been considerably secularized. Non-Biblical and strongly comic elements were gradually introduced: Noah's wife, for example, became a great comic character, drunken and shrewish; "ranting Herod" became an enjoyable scarecrow. But in spite of these secular qualities, the plays remained basically didactic and pious. They were an attempt to domesticate Biblical history, to make events that took place a very long time ago in a remote country seem real and convincing to a medieval audience; this is an aspect that is difficult for moderns to appreciate.

Nevertheless, the best of the miracle plays are very good dramatic literature. Their merit lies not so much in the dialogue − in the best plays the dialogue is often brilliant or moving, but more often seems stiff and awkward − but rather in the dramatic architecture, in the building up of effective scenes for the stage. Anyone who has seen a well-acted production of *The Second Shepherds' Play,* for example, will attest to the wonderful skill of its movement and structure. The success of a recent television production of several plays of the Chester cycle is further proof that these dramas, even now, have real power on the stage − they are hilarious, moving, and impressive works of art. All of the authors of these plays are anonymous, as might be expected. Most probably the plays of each cycle were gradually built up over the generations, new plays added from time to time, older ones revised or expanded. The only "author" who can be identified is himself nameless, the "Wakefield Master" who worked in the first part of the fifteenth century, and who has been solely credited with five or six of the best plays of the Wakefield cycle and probably rewrote half a dozen others. Whoever he was, the Wakefield Master possessed fine dramatic and stylistic talents, and deserves to be ranked as the first great comic dramatist in our language.

A very different type of medieval drama, the "morality play" is a later development, the earliest fragment in English dating about 1400. Whereas the miracle play is a dramatization of an episode from religious history, the morality is a kind of dramatized sermon in which forces of good and evil contend for the possession of man's soul. The characters are not individual persons as in the miracle play, but are personified abstractions in a moral allegory. Characters like "Mankind" or "Everyman," for example, stand for the whole of the human race, every man and woman in the world. Only four such plays have survived in Middle English − *The Pride of Life* (c. 1400), *The Castle of Perserverance* (c. 1475), *Mankind* (c. 1475), and *Everyman* (c. 1500), a fact that suggests that the morality play was far less popular in England than the miracle play, though the morality persisted well into the sixteenth century and contributed in a very important way to the birth of the Elizabethan drama.

The longest and most elaborate of the mortality plays is *The Castle of Perseverance,* the manuscript of which includes a diagram for its staging. The diagram shows a circular theatre with the Castle in the center and other scaffolds around the perimeter symbolizing God, the World, the Flesh, the Devil, and Covetousness. In his pilgrimage through life the central character, Mankind, moves from one scaffold to another as he is pulled in various directions by evil or virtuous forces. In the end, of course, Mankind is saved by the mercy of God. Whereas this complex play is wholly serious in tone, *Mankind* is very different, containing large elements of comic and even obscene horseplay revolving around the grotesque devil, Titivillus, and his attendant "vices." The low comedy tends to overwhelm the serious moral lesson in this play.

Artistically, by far the greatest of the morality plays in *Everyman,* a powerful dramatization of the Christian death. The dramatic structure here is spare and tight, with a series of memorable scenes showing Everyman as he moves inexorably toward the grave. Not a word is wasted, the scenes are skillfully organized for visual effects, the dialogue is starkly eloquent, and the play as a whole has the feeling of inevitability that is a sign of high art. The characters in *Everyman,* moreover, are not empty abstractions: each is portrayed strongly and satisfyingly as a distinct personality. At the same time, most of the characters other than Everyman are extensions of various parts of Everyman's own personality. Fellowship, for example, represents Everyman's love for social conniviality; Cousin and Kindred stand for Everyman's family pride and dependence upon blood relationships;

Goods, of course, is Everyman's lust for material wealth; Knowledge is his understanding of the prescribed means of salvation; Five Wits are his own physical senses; and so forth. Consequently, the dramatic conflict in this play is an *internal* one, a struggle within Everyman between good and evil aspects of his own character as he moves toward death. The end result is enormously impressive in its spiritual and dramatic potency. With the possible exception of *The Second Shepherds' Play* of the Wakefield Master, *Everyman* is unquestionably the supreme achievement of the medieval drama in England.

EARLY TUDOR LITERATURE

Historically, the early Tudor period extends from the accession of the first Tudor monarch, Henry VII, in 1485 to the accession of the last and greatest of that name, Elizabeth I, in 1558. In terms of creative literature in all genres this era (except in Scotland in the earlier part of it) is singularly barren. The fact is the more suprising since we are accustomed to thinking of early Tudor times as the beginning of the Renaissance in England, when the floodgates of the "New Learning," the rediscovery of ancient Roman and Greek culture, finally opened and stimulating (even revolutionary) influences poured in from the Continent. At the same time the introduction of the printing press, first established by William Caxton in 1476, resulted in a rapid increase of the literacy rate and provided undreamed of new opportunities for writers. But this new world was very slow in producing native literary fruits; for generations England seemed to be simply *absorbing* and gradually adjusting to the new influences, rather than creating. It is significant that what was probably the greatest single work of creative imagination during the entire period, Sir Thomas More's *Utopia,* was written not in English but in Latin. New writing in English, though copious, was for the most part mediocre, and not at all revolutionary, fully justifying C. S. Lewis's designation of the period as the "Drab Age." Medieval attitudes and practices persisted for generations in the Renaissance, giving way only very slowly and grudgingly to the changes that eventually led to the great flowering of English literature and culture in the golden age of Elizabeth.

Prose

Thanks to the printing press, early Tudor prose is very voluminous, but the great bulk of it is polemical, didactic, derivative, and dull. Even the better examples of it, such as Sir Thomas Elyot's *Book of the Governor* (1531) or some of the writings of More, or Latimer, or Ascham, though they are interesting as historical, religious, or cultural documents, have little value as literary art. Two shining exceptions to this generalization, however, must be made: the Bible translations of William Tyndale (1525–30) and Miles Coverdale (1535) and the *Book of Common Prayer* (1549). Tyndale, in particular, deserves an honored place in the history of English prose. Not only is his translation of the New Testament and of the first five books of the Old a work of remarkable pioneering scholarship (the first English versions to be based directly on the Greek and Hebrew texts rather than on the Latin Vulgate), it is also a work of great literary excellence. Tyndale's prose is clear, rhythmical, and vigorous – the most beautiful in our language since Malory's – and that of his friend Coverdale is almost as good. Together, Tyndale and Coverdale laid down a magnificent stylistic basis for the great King James Bible of 1611. The splendid Anglican *Book of Common Prayer,* also mainly a translation (from Latin) and chiefly the work of Archbishop Thomas Cranmer, is another esthetic gem in the dreary welter of early Tudor prose.

Poetry

In poetry the accomplishment of this period is somewhat better, though far from dazzling. Over a span of nearly seventy-five years, only four poets of substantial talent appeared – Skelton, Wyatt, Surrey, and Lyndsay – amidst a host of lesser lights. The earliest of the gifted Tudor poets, John Skelton, was an eccentric and limited kind of genius. His earlier poems are medieval and conventional in style, though the best of them, *The Bowge* [wages] *of Court,* a satiric dream-vision depicting the corruption and madness of court life, has passages of real brilliance. Skelton is best remembered, however, for his later work in a strange, chaotic verse form, the "Skeltonic," consisting of short lines of two or three stresses each (usually) and an indefinite number of unaccented syllables, combined with obsessive rhyming – ranging from couplets to series of three, four, five or more consecutive rhyming lines. This loose, almost childlike form can be amazingly effective when Skelton is writing on light or comic subjects as he is in *Philip Sparrow* and *The Tunnyng of Elinour Rummyng,* but it fails disastrously when used as a vehicle for weightier themes. Skelton at his best is curiously attractive as a kind of madcap poet; he is a bold experimenter, and as such he fits the Renaissance stereotype better than most of his era. But he falls short of genuine greatness as a comic writer because of the limitations not only of his wild methods but also of his imaginative sympathies.

Sir Thomas Wyatt was also an eccentric, but of a very different kind. His importance does not lie in his introduction of Petrarchan love poetry into England. As a matter of fact, Petrarchan influences had been seeping into English poetry for a long time before Wyatt (Chaucer, after all, was also a "Petrarchan"), and continued to do so after his time. The great Petrarchan love poetry of the Elizabethan golden age would have developed even if Wyatt had never existed. Wyatt's intrinsic importance and his glory lie in the powerfully personal style that he developed while working within conventional forms, those of the medieval English lyric, or of the Petrarchan sonnet. At its best, Wyatt's style is original, direct, spare, and unadorned; it has little of the mellifluous sweetness of Petrarch, but does have a strange, stark power of its own. Within his fairly narrow range Wyatt is inimitable; his grave, tormented utterance makes him one of the fine love poets in our literature. On the whole, Wyatt is a stronger and more original poet than his younger friend Henry Howard, Earl of Surrey. Surrey, of course, has historical importance for his skillful exploitation of the Italian sonnet and for his invention of blank verse as a vehicle for his translation of the first two books of Virgil's *Aeneid.* Though Surrey is a smooth and accomplished poet, he lacks force. His rendering of Virgil, for example, looks pale and "academic" when compared to the colorful vigor of Gavin Douglas. But the form he created, blank verse, was highly admired by the Elizabethans, and probably he determined the choice of that medium by incomparably greater poets – Marlowe, Shakespeare, Milton – and that is no small distinction.

Sir David Lyndsay might logically been treated in the section on Middle Scots poetry, since he is the last major figure among the Scots makers and is also largely medieval in his attitudes, but the lateness of his dates makes it more convenient to consider him with the early Tudor writers. Like Dunbar before him, Lyndsay was a court poet (under James IV and V), but unlike Dunbar he was a vehement reformer and propagandist for change. The bulk of Lyndsay's poetry, including his dramatic masterpiece *A Satire of the Three Estates,* consists of eloquent pleas for reform and regeneration of both church and state in Scotland. Couched in the standard medieval forms of dream-vision, debate, or moral allegory, Lyndsay's political poems are modern in the urgency of their messages, and because he was on the side of the future his work became hugely popular in Scotland. He is not a great poet, but is always sound and competent, almost never dull. Artistically the finest of his non-dramatic work is the delightful tale of *Squire Meldrum* which, alone among Lyndsay's poems, has no political lesson to teach – it is pure, rollicking fun.

Of the minor poets of the early Tudor period little need be said. Stephen Hawes, who served in the court of Henry VII, was in general a dull Lydgatian sort of poet who often lacked even the competence of Lydgate. Alexander Barclay, author of the long, satiric *Ship of Fools* and of *Eclogues,* is scarcely better. He is mainly derivative, translating mediocre Latin works into clumsy English. Many of the contributors to Tottel's *Miscellany* (1557), the earliest major anthology of Tudor verse, are far more skillful than Hawes or Barclay. Poets like Lord Vaux, for example, are smooth and deft, but their work is limited to short, conventional lyrics, lacking in scope, passion, or genuine distinction. Early Tudor poetry, on the whole, is less than exciting. The influence of the New Learning tended for a long time to be stultifying rather than envigorating, and with the exception of a small handful of good poets the record of this era is clearly mediocre and disappointing. It gives almost no hint of the sudden, miraculous blossoming that was to come in the second half of the reign of Queen Elizabeth.

Drama

The two basic types of English drama in the late Middle Ages, the miracle and the morality play, continued to flourish well into the sixteenth century. But the morality tradition in particular underwent important changes that were to be crucial to the development of Elizabethan drama. In early Tudor times the morality moved away from the didactic universality of *The Castle of Perserverance* or *Everyman* and became a vehicle for the dramatizing of very specific contemporary issues in religion and politics. Skelton's huge morality play, *Magnificence,* for example, is largely a piece of propaganda in support of the Tudor monarchy. Similarly, Lyndsay's *Satire of the Three Estates,* is focussed directly upon the problems of Scotland in the reign of James V. This sprawling play (the full text must have taken about six hours to perform) is dramatically the finest of the old-fashioned moralities of the Tudor era and has been revived recently with great success.

The Tudor history play and the "interlude" both evolved out of the morality tradition. John Bale in *King John* combined the personified abstractions of the medieval heritage with actual historical persons and events, and in so doing he provided a precedent for the full-blown historical plays of Shakespeare and other Elizabethans half a century later. The Tudor "interlude" was a specialized kind of morality play which centered upon some topical argument in religion or politics. The pioneering interludes of John Rastell, especially *Gentylnes and Nobylyte,* tend to be dramatized "debates" that are more didactic than dramatic. These short plays were made to serve as entertainments at festive banquets. Rastell's successor, John Heywood, was the most prolific author of interludes, the best of which is *The Play of the Weather.* Though all of Heywood's plays are occasionally enlivened by humorous (sometimes bawdy) scenes, on the whole they are dramatically weak: the "lesson" predominates over theatrical effect. Though none of these Tudor extensions of the morality tradition comes close to equalling the stunning power of *Everyman,* they did provide a crucial bridge between the medieval genre and the great Elizabethan drama, where the influence of the morality play with its good-evil conflict is most obvious in Marlowe's *Dr. Faustus* and in several of the works of Shakespeare.

The early Tudor period also saw the beginning of the revolutionary impact of Roman and Greek drama upon the English theatre. The Roman comedies of Terence and Plautus, at least, became known during this era, though the full influence of Roman and Greek tragedy did not become operative until the reign of Elizabeth. One of Terence's plays had been translated by Rastell as early as the 1530's, and by about 1540 the dramatic structure and comic stereotypes of both Terence and Plautus had borne native English fruit in the work of Nicholas Udall. His *Ralph Roister Doister* employs Terence's five-act scheme that became the standard model for the Elizabethans, and bases its two main characters upon figures in two separate plays by the Roman dramatist. As a consequence, *Ralph Roister Doister* is the first English comedy to approach the fullness and complexity of the Elizabethan plays. It has an amusing plot and some lively scenes. The influence of the Roman drama is here especially important in terms of structure: Terence and Plautus and, a little later, Seneca and the Greeks, bequeathed to the English theatre a sense of dramatic plot structure that was clearer and tighter and, at the same time, more complex than had ever been known in the native traditions.

Intrinsically, the quality of early Tudor drama is not very impressive. Not a single play of this era can match the dramatic skill and intensity the greatest examples of late medieval miracle or morality plays. Nevertheless, the Tudor drama has importance and interest as the seedbed out of which grew the supreme dramatic achievements in our literature. In it we see slowly evolving all three of the strands that finally come together in the magic fusion of the Elizabethan golden age. From the vital and continuing tradition of the miracle plays came the kind of physical stage and acting conventions that governed Shakespeare's theatre, together with some old native English character types and comic effects. From the morality plays, through the Tudor interludes, came the essential element of dramatic conflict between forces of good and evil. Finally, from the classical Roman drama as rediscovered and exploited by the Tudor dramatists emerged a new and salutary sense of order and structure, as well as some further stimulating character types. In the 1580's and 1590's all three of these traditions were destined to merge in the rich amalgam of the Elizabethan drama.

READING LIST

1. Bibliographies, handbooks, etc.

Geddie, W., *Bibliography of Middle Scots Poems,* 1912.

Wells, J. E., *A Manual of Writings in Middle English 1050–1400,* 1916; 9 supplements through 1951; revised edition by J. B. Severs, 1967–

Lawrence, W. W., *Selected Bibliography of Medieval Literature in English,* 1930.

Pinto, V. de Sola, editor, *The English Renaissance 1510–1688,* 1938; revised edition, 1966.

Loomis, R. S., *Introduction to Medieval Literature Chiefly in English: A Reading List and Bibliography,* 1939; revised edition, 1948.

Harbage, Alfred, B., *Annals of English Drama 975–1700,* 1940; revised edition by Samuel Schoenbaum, 1964; supplements, 1966, 1970.

Brown, Carleton, and R. H. Robbins, editors, *Index of Middle English Verse,* 1943; supplement edited by Robbins and J. L. Cutler, 1965.

Farrar, C. P., and A. P. Evans, *Bibliography of English Translations from Medieval Sources,* 1946.

Stratman, Carl J., *Bibliography of Medieval Drama,* 1954; revised edition, 1972.

Bonser, W., *An Anglo-Saxon and Celtic Bibliography 450–1087,* 2 vols., 1957.

Ker, N. R., *Catalogue of Manuscripts Containing Anglo-Saxon,* 1957.

Morrell, M. C., *A Manual of Old English Biblical Materials,* 1965.

Lievsay, J. L., *The Sixteenth Century: Skelton Through Hooker,* 1968.

Levine, Mortimer, *Tudor England 1485–1603,* 1968.

Robinson, Fred Colson, *Old English Literature: A Select Bibliography,* 1970.

2. General histories

Chambers, E. K., *The Medieval Stage,* 2 vols., 1903.

Ker, W. P., *English Literature: Medieval,* 1912.

Renwick, W. L., and H. Orton, *The Beginnings of English Literature to Skelton,* 1939; revised edition, 1952; revised edition by M. F. Wakelin, 1966.

Atkins, J. W. H., *English Literary Criticism: The Medieval Phase,* 1943; *The Renaissance,* 1947.

Anderson, G. K., *The Literature of the Anglo-Saxons,* 1949; revised edition, 1966.

Anderson, G. K., *Old and Middle English Literature from the Beginnings to 1485,* 1950.

Kane, George, *Middle English Literature,* 1951.

Rossiter, A. P., *English Drama from Early Times to the Elizabethans,* 1951.

Wilson, R. M., *The Lost Literature of Medieval England,* 1952; revised edition, 1970.

Betherum, Dorothy, editor, *Critical Approaches to Medieval Literature*, 1959.
Williams, A., *The Drama of Medieval England*, 1961.
Zesmer, David M., *Guide to English Literature from Beowulf Through Chaucer and Medieval Drama*, 1961.
Spearing, A. C., *Criticism and Medieval Poetry*, 1964; revised edition, 1972.
Lewis, C. S., *The Discarded Image: An Introduction to Medieval and Renaissance Literature*, 1964.
Greenfield, Stanley B., *A Critical History of Old English Literature*, 1965.
Schlauch, Margaret, *English Medieval Literature and Its Social Foundations*, 1965.
Jackson, W. T. H., *Medieval Literature*, 1966.
Wrenn, C. L., *A Study of Old English Literature*, 1967.
Matthews, William, *Old and Middle English Literature*, 1968.
Dronke, Peter, *The Medieval Lyric*, 1968.
Fowler, D. C., *A Literary History of the Popular Ballad*, 1968.
Selz, W. A., editor, *Medieval Drama*, 1968.
Kinghorn, A. M., *Medieval Drama*, 1968.
Taylor, J., and A. H. Nelson, editors, *Medieval English Drama: Essays Critical and Contextual*, 1972.
Shippey, T. A., *Old English Verse*, 1972.
Sticca, S., editor, *The Medieval Drama*, 1972.
Pearsall, Derek, *Old English and Middle English Poetry*, 1977.

3. Topics, themes, short periods, etc.
Brooke, Tucker, *The Tudor Drama*, 1912.
Berdan, J. M., *Early Tudor Poetry 1485–1547*, 1920.
Patch, H. R., *The Goddess Fortuna in Medieval Literature*, 1927.
Taylor, A. B., *An Introduction to Medieval Romance*, 1930.
Gerould, G. H., *The Ballad of Tradition*, 1932.
Patch, H. R., *The Tradition of Boethius*, 1935.
Lewis, C. S., *The Allegory of Love: A Study in Medieval Tradition*, 1936.
Baldwin, C. S., *Renaissance Literary Theory and Practice 1400–1600*, 1939.
Fisher, F., *Narrative Art in Medieval Romances*, 1939.
Wilson, R. M., *Early Middle English Literature*, 1939; revised edition, 1968.
Speirs, John, *The Scots Literary Tradition*, 1940; revised edition, 1962.
Gardiner, H. C., *Mysteries' End: An Investigation of the Last Days of the Medieval Religious Stage*, 1946.
Bennett, H. S., *Chaucer and the Fifteenth Century*, 1947.
Moore, A. K., *The Secular Lyric in Middle English*, 1951.
Sisam, Kenneth, *Studies in the History of Old English Literature*, 1953.
Lewis, C. S., *English Literature in the Sixteenth Century, Excluding Drama*, 1954.
Chambers, E. K., *English Literature at the Close of the Middle Ages*, 1954.
Evans, Maurice, *English Poetry in the 16th Century*, 1955; revised edition, 1967.
Kinsley, James, editor, *Scottish Poetry: A Critical Survey*, 1955.
Everett, Dorothy, *Essays on Middle English Literature*, 1955.
Craig, Hardin, *English Religious Drama of the Middle Ages*, 1955.
Speirs, John, *Medieval English Poetry: The Non-Chaucerian Tradition*, 1957.
Craik, T. W., *The Tudor Interlude*, 1958.
Wittig, Kurt, *The Scottish Tradition in Literature*, 1958.
Campbell, L. B., *Divine Poetry and Drama in 16th-Century England*, 1959.
Mason, H. A., *Humanism and Poetry in the Early Tudor Period*, 1959.
Wickham, Glynne, *Early English Stages 1300–1600*, vol. 1, 1959.
Loomis, R. S., editor, *Arthurian Literature in the Middle Ages*, 1959.
Prosser, Eleanor, *Drama and Religion in the English Mystery Plays: A Re-Evaluation*, 1961.
Stevens, J. E., *Music and Poetry in the Early Tudor Court 1480–1530*, 1961.

Barber, Richard, *Arthur of Albion: An Introduction to the Arthurian Literature and Legends of England,* 1961.
Bevington, David M., *From Mankind to Marlowe,* 1962.
Manning, S., *Wisdom and Number: Toward a Critical Appraisal of the Middle English Religious Lyric,* 1962.
Bliss, A. J., *An Introduction to Old English Metre,* 1962.
Loomis, R. S., *The Development of Arthurian Romance,* 1963.
Schlauch, Margaret, *Antecedents of the English Novel 1400–1600,* 1963.
Hardison, O. B., Jr., *Christian Rite and Christian Drama in the Middle Ages,* 1965.
Matthews, William, editor, *Medieval Secular Literature: Four Essays,* 1965.
Vasta, Ed., editor, *Middle English Survey: Critical Essays,* 1965.
Brewer, D. S., *Chaucer and Chaucerians,* 1966.
Cosman, M. P., *The Education of the Hero in Arthurian Romance,* 1966.
Tuve, Rosamond, *Allegorical Imagery: Some Medieval Books and Their Posterity,* 1966.
Vinaver, Eugène, *Form and Meaning in Medieval Romance,* 1966.
Howard, Donald R., *The Three Temptations: Medieval Man in Search of the World,* 1966.
Stanley, E. G., editor, *Continuations and Beginnings: Studies in Old English Literature,* 1966.
Peterson, Douglas L., *The English Lyric from Wyatt to Donne: A History of the Plain and Eloquent Styles,* 1967.
Hieatt, Constance B., *The Realism of Dream Visions,* 1967.
Creed, R. P., editor, *Old English Poetry: Fifteen Essays,* 1967.
Pineas, R., *Tudor Drama and Politics,* 1968.
Woolf, Rosemary, *The English Religious Lyric in the Middle Ages,* 1968.
Newman, F. X., editor, *The Meaning of Courtly Love,* 1968.
Bessinger, Jess B., Jr., and Stanley J. Kahrl, editors, *Essential Articles for the Study of Old English Poetry,* 1968.
Isaacs, Neil D., *Structural Principles in Old English Poetry,* 1968.
Wilson, F. P., *The English Drama 1485–1584,* 1969.
Watts, Ann Chalmers, *The Lyre and the Harp: A Comparative Reconsideration of Oral Tradition in Homer and Old English Epic Poetry,* 1969.
Owen, D. D. R., editor, *Arthurian Romance: Seven Essays,* 1970.
Loomis, R. S., *Studies in Medieval Literature,* 1970.
Bloomfield, Morton W., *Essays and Explorations,* 1970.
Barber, Richard, *The Knight and Chivalry,* 1970.
Huppé, Bernard F., *The Web of Words,* 1970.
Clemoes, P., *Rhythm and Cosmic Order in Old English Christian Literature,* 1970.
Brody, A., *The English Mummers and Their Plays: Traces of Ancient Mysteries,* 1971.
Burrow, John A., *Ricardian Poetry: Chaucer, Gower, Lydgate, and the "Gawain" Poet,* 1971.
Aitken, A. J., Angus McIntosh, and Hermann Palsson, editors, *Edinburgh Studies in English and Scots,* 1971.
Vinaver, Eugène, *The Rise of Romance,* 1971.
Gradon, P. O. E., *Form and Style in Early English Literature,* 1971.
Piehler, P., *The Visionary Landscape: A Study of Medieval Allegory,* 1971.
Greenfield, Stanley B., *The Interpretation of Old English Poems,* 1972.
Lindsay, Maurice, *History of Scottish Literature,* 1977.

4. Anthologies of primary works

Child, F. J., editor, *The English and Scottish Popular Ballads,* 8 vols., 1857–59, 5 vols., 1882–98; abridged edition, edited by H. C. Sargent and G. L. Kittredge, 1904.
Sweet, Henry, *An Anglo-Saxon Reader,* 1876; revised edition by Dorothy Whitelock, 1967.
Miracle Plays:
  The Digby Plays, edited by F. J. Furnivall, 1882.
  York Plays, edited by L. T. Smith, 1885; edited by J. S. Purvis, 1957.

Chester Plays, edited by R. M. Lumiansky and David Mills, 1974.

Towneley Plays, edited by G. England and A. W. Pollard, 1897; edited by M. Rose, 1961; see also the entry for the Wakefield Master.

Ludus Coventriae, edited by K. S. Black, 1922; edited by R. T. Davies, 1972.

Non-Cycle Plays and Fragments, edited by Norman Davies, 1970.

Bright, J. W., *An Anglo-Saxon Reader*, 1891; revised edition, edited by J. R. Hulbert and B. C. Monroe, 1965; the poems in the reader edited by F. P. Magoun, Jr., 1967.

Sommer, H. O., editor, *Vulgate Versions of the Arthurian Romances*, 8 vols., 1908–16.

Pollard, A. W., editor, *Fifteenth-Century Verse and Prose*, 1912.

McKnight, G. H., editor, *Middle English Humorous Tales in Verse*, 1913.

Hall, J., editor, *Selections from Early Middle English 1130–1250*, 2 vols., 1920; revised edition, 1949–51.

Sisam, Kenneth, editor, *Fourteenth-Century Verse and Prose*, 1921.

Chambers, E. K., and F. Sidgwick, editors, *Early English Lyrics*, 1921.

Adams, J. Q., editor, *Chief Pre-Shakespearean Dramas*, 1924.

Brown, Carleton, editor, *Religious Lyrics of the XIVth Century*, 1924; revised edition, edited by G. V. Smithers, 1952.

Hammond, E. P., editor, *English Verse Between Chaucer and Surrey*, 1927.

Krapp, G. P., and E. V. K. Dobbie, editors, *The Anglo-Saxon Poetry Records*, 6 vols., 1931–53.

Chambers, E. K., editor, *The Oxford Book of Sixteenth-Century Verse*, 1932.

Brown, Carleton, editor, *English Lyrics of the XIIIth Century*, 1932.

Young, Karl, editor, *The Drama of the Medieval Church*, 1933.

Gray, M. M., editor, *Scottish Poetry from Barbour to James VI*, 1935.

Neilson, W. W., and K. G. T. Webster, editors, *The Chief British Poets of the Fourteenth and Fifteenth Centuries: Selected Poems*, 1936.

Brown, Carleton, editor, *Religious Lyrics of the Fifteenth Century*, 1939.

Loomis, R. S., and H. W. Wells, editors, *Representative Medieval and Tudor Plays*, 1942.

Loomis, R. S., and R. Willard, editors, *Medieval English Verse and Poetry*, 1948.

Dickens, B., and R. M. Wilson, editors, *Early Middle English Reader*, 1951.

Robbins, R. H., editor, *Secular Lyrics of the XIVth and XVth Centuries*, 1952; revised edition, 1955.

Rollins, E. M., and H. Baker, Jr., editors, *The Renaissance in England: Non-Dramatic Prose and Verse of the 16th Century*, 1954.

Nugent, E. M., editor, *The Thought and Culture of the English Renaissance: An Anthology of Tudor Prose 1487–1555*, 1955.

Lehnert, M., editor, *Poetry and Prose of the Anglo-Saxons*, 2 vols., 1955–56; revised edition, 1960–69.

Cawley, A. C., editor, *Everyman and Medieval Miracle Plays*, 1956; revised edition, 1957.

Loomis, R. S., and L. H., editors, *Medieval Romances*, 1957.

Robbins, R. H., editor, *Historical Poems of the XIVth and XVth Centuries*, 1959.

Matthews, William, editor, *Later Medieval English Prose*, 1962.

Davies, R. T., editor, *Medieval English Lyrics: A Critical Anthology*, 1963.

Zall, Paul M., editor, *A Hundred Merry Tales and Other English Jestbooks of the Fifteenth and Sixteenth Centuries*, 1963.

Bolton, W. F., editor, *An Introduction to Old English*, 1963; revised edition, 1966.

Gassner, John, editor, *Medieval and Tudor Drama*, 1963.

Brengle, R. L., editor, *Arthur, King of Britain: History, Romance, Chronicle, and Criticism, with Texts in Modern English from Gildas to Malory*, 1964.

Stone, Brian, editor, *Medieval English Verse*, 1965.

Hodgart, M. J. C., editor, *The Faber Book of Ballads*, 1965.

Thomas, R. G., editor, *Ten Miracle Plays*, 1966.

Gibbs, A. C., editor, *Middle English Romances*, 1966.

Sands, Donald B., editor, *Middle English Verse Romances*, 1966.

Bennett, J. A. W., and G. V. Smithers, editors, *Early Middle English Verse and Prose,* 1966; revised edition, 1968.

MacQueen, John, and Tom Scott, editors, *The Oxford Book of Scottish Verse,* 1966.

Fowler, R. G., editor, *Old English Prose and Verse,* 1966.

Scott, Tom, editor, *Late Medieval Scots Poetry,* 1967.

Stevick, R. D., editor, *Five Middle English Narratives,* 1967.

Kinsley, James, editor, *The Oxford Book of Ballads,* 1969.

Hamer, R. F. S., editor, *A Choice of Anglo-Saxon Verse,* 1970.

Kinghorn, A. M., editor, *The Middle Scots Poets,* 1970.

Tydeman, William M., editor, *English Poetry 1400–1580,* 1970.

Sisam, Celia and Kenneth, editors, *The Oxford Book of Medieval English Verse,* 1970.

Owen, Lewis J., and Nancy H. Owen, editors, *Middle English Poetry: An Anthology,* 1971.

Dunn, Charles W., and Edward T. Byrnes, editors, *Middle English Literature,* 1973.

Gray, Douglas, editor, *A Selection of Religious Lyrics,* 1975.

Greene, Richard L., editor, *The Early English Carols,* 1976.

BALE, John. English. Born in Cove, near Dunwich, Suffolk, 21 November 1495. Entered the Carmelite Monastery, Norwich: educated there, and at Jesus College, Cambridge; converted to Protestantism by the teaching of Lord Wentworth, and renounced his monastic vows. Married to Dorothy Bale; several children. Rector of Thornden, Suffolk; also in the service of Thomas Cromwell: led an acting troupe at Cromwell's behest, 1537–40, and wrote propaganda for him; after Cromwell's death, lived in Germany, 1540 until the accession of Edward VI, 1547; appointed Rector of Bishopstoke, Hampshire; Vicar of Swaffham, 1551; Bishop of Ossory in Ireland, 1552–53; after the accession of Mary, lived on the Continent, 1553 until the accession of Elizabeth, 1558; returned to England: Prebendary at Canterbury, 1560–63. *Died in November 1563.*

PUBLICATIONS

Collections

    Select Works, edited by Henry Christmas. 1849.
    Dramatic Writings, edited by John S. Farmer. 1907.

Plays

    King John (produced ?). 1538; edited by William A. Armstrong, in *English History Plays,* 1965.
    The Chief Promises of God unto Man (produced ?). 1545(?); edited by Ernest Rhys, in *Everyman and Other Interludes,* 1909.
    The Temptation of Our Lord (produced ?). 1548(?); edited by P. Schwemmer, 1919.
    Three Laws, of Nature, Moses, and Christ, Corrupted by Sodomites, Pharisees, and Papists (produced ?). 1548(?).
    John Baptist (produced ?). In *Harleian Miscellany 1,* 1774.

Verse

    An Answer to a Papistical Exhortation. 1548(?); edited by H. Hugh, in *Fugitive Tracts in Verse 1,* 1875.

Other

    A Brief Chronicle Concerning Sir John Oldcastle, the Lord Cobham. 1544.
    The Acts of English Votaries. 1546; revised edition, 1548.
    The Examination of Anne Askewe. 2 vols., 1546–47.
    The Image of Both Churches after the Revelation of St. John. 1548(?).
    Illustrium Majoris Britanniae Scriptorum Summarium. 1548; revised edition, as *Scriptorum Illustrium Majoris Britanniae Catalogus,* 2 vols., 1557–59; notebook edited by R. L. Poole and M. Bateson, as *Index Britanniae Scriptorum,* 1902.
    The Apology of Bale Against a Rank Papist. 1555(?).
    Acta Romanorum Pontificum. 1558.
    A Declaration Concerning the Clergy of London. 1561.

    Editor, *A Treatise unto Henry VIII,* by John Lambert. 1548(?).

Translator, *The True History of the Christian Departing of Martin Luther,* by Justus Jonas. 1546.

Bibliography: *A Bibliography of Bale* by William T. Davies, 1947.

Reading List: *Bale: A Study in the Minor Literature of the Reformation* by Jesse W. Harris, 1940; *Bale, Dramatist and Antiquary* by Honor MacCusker, 1942; *The Plays of Bale* by Thora B. Blatt, 1968; *Mittelälterliche Tradition und Reformatorische Polemik in den Spielen Bales* by Klaus Sperk, 1973; *Bale, Mythmaker for the English Reformation* by Leslie P. Fairfield, 1976.

*   *   *

John Bale, Bishop of Ossory, was the first English writer to use the drama for polemical purposes, inveighing against the "heap of adders of Antichrist's generation" (*King John*) and urging his audiences, as he urged congregations, to turn away from the practices of Roman Catholicism and towards an orthodoxy that recognized the king as God's deputy on earth and sole representative of the Amighty as head of His church. No Christian doctrine was infallible, he taught, unless it was grounded in Holy Scripture.

Of some twenty-one dramas that Bale is believed to have written, only five survive; and these five, one alone, *King John*, is readily available and of interest to students of the drama both for its intrinsic merit and for its unique position mid-way between the Morality Play and the historical dramas of the Elizabethans. The spur for Bale's writing of *King John* may have been provided by a remark of William Tyndale's in his *Obedience of a Christian Man* (1528); Tyndale invited his readers to "Consider the story of King John, where I doubt not but they [the Catholic historians] have put the best and fairest for themselves, and the worst for King John." Bale repeats the charge in his play:

> You priests are the cause that chronicles doth defame
> So many princes and men of notable name;
> For you take upon you to write them evermore;
> And, therefore, King John is like to rue it sore.

The play shows John at his most protestant, defending Widow England against the powers of Sedition, Private Wealth, Cardinal Pandulphus, and the Pope. England is widowed, she tells the king, because "These vile popish swine" have driven her husband into exile; her husband is no less than "God himself, the spouse of every sort/That seek him in faith to the soul's health and comfort." Although John has the authority of the Bible for all his actions, he is nevertheless forced to capitulate to Rome; but he does so with the resignation of a martyr:

> As God shall judge me, I do not this of cowardness,
> But of compassion in this extreme heaviness.
> Shall my people shed their blood in such habundance?
> Nay! I shall rather give up my whole governance.

King John dies of poison, administered by Simon of Swinsett; but the play does not end here. In a final scene Verity addresses Clergy, Nobility, and Civil Order, pointing out their failings and the king's virtues until, in the presence of Imperial Majesty, she exacts a new declaration of faith and intent: "We detest the Pope, and abhor him to the fiend." Imperial Majesty is then advised how best to maintain supreme power, and the play ends with a hymn of praise. Bale probably wrote his first version c. 1538, but revised and added to it throughout his life; it may well have been performed on the occasion of Queen Elizabeth's visit to Ipswich in 1561.

In the figures of King John himself, Stephen Langton, and Cardinal Pandulphus, Bale is presenting individuals, their characteristics supplied by the chronicles (although adapted, when necessary, to suit the dramatist's didactic purpose). But the unashamed abstractions of Clergy, Private Wealth, Dissimulation, and Nobility set the play securely in the Morality tradition. Sedition is the Morality's Vice, at best a comic nuisance and at worst the devil's advocate. Impartial satire is vested in the Vice: Sedition, although he claims to support the pope, is an eloquent exponent of the Roman church's false relics:

> Here is first a bone of the blessed Trinity,
> A dram of the turd of sweet Saint Barnaby.
> Here is a feather of good Saint Michael's wing,
> A tooth of Saint Twyde, a piece of David's harp string,
> The good blood of Hales, and our blessed Lady's milk;
> A louse of Saint Francis in this same crimson silk.

With this combination of the real and the allegorical in his *dramatis personae*, Bale shows himself a master of theatricality. He has arranged his dialogue so that nineteen speaking parts can be performed by nine actors – a necessity often forced upon the small travelling companies who acted the Morality Plays. But Bale extracts a virtue from this necessity: the real and the allegorical fuse – as in this stage direction: "Here go out Usurped Power and Private Wealth and Sedition: Usurped Power shall dress for the Pope: Private Wealth for a Cardinal; and Sedition for a Monk." That the transformations were intended to be noticed by the audience is clear from King John's observation when Sedition enters, this time dressed as the bishop, Stephen Langton: "Methink[s] this bishop resembleth much Sedition."

The language of *King John* is simple, but Bale achieves a variety of tones, from the moving pleas of Widow England to the dignified oratory of Imperial Majesty. Most notable of all is the racy colloquialism, contained within the blank verse line, of the speeches of Sedition; here Bale shows himself to be not only the inheritor of the Morality tradition and its Vice, but also the precursor of the Elizabethan history play with its Falstaff.

—Roma Gill

BARBOUR, John.   Scottish.   Born near Aberdeen in 1316. May have studied at Oxford University and in Paris, and travelled extensively on the Continent. Took holy orders; Archdeacon of Aberdeen, 1357–95; also held office in the household of King Robert II: auditor of exchequer, 1372, 1382, 1384; clerk for the audit of the household, 1374; pensioned by the king, 1378. *Died 13 March 1395.*

PUBLICATIONS

Verse

The Bruce, edited by J. Pinkerton.   3 vols., 1790.
The Bruce, edited by W. W. Skeat.   4 vols., 1870–89.

The Bruce, edited by W. M. Mackenzie. 1909.
The Bruce: A Selection, edited by Alexander Kinghorn. 1960.
The Bruce (translation), by A. A. H. Douglas. 1964.

Reading List: *The Wallace and the Bruce Restudied* by J. T. T. Brown, 1900; *Barbour, Poet and Translator* by George Neilson, 1900; *Die Nationale Literatur Schottlands* by Friedrich Brie, 1937.

*   *   *

John Barbour is the father of Scottish poetry, yet his *Bruce*, materially a chronological series of heroic narratives, derives from a native tradition of lays in the French octosyllabic couplet that is probably as old as the century of Malcolm Canmore and Macbeth. As in the lays the matter is factual, the treatment dramatic and spirited, but with a political perspective and descriptive fluency learned respectively from Scottish histories and French romances. He knew nothing of his English contemporary Chaucer.

Generally Barbour's subject is national and individual freedom – "Fredome is a noble thing,/It makis man to have liking,/He lives at ese that frely lives." His purpose is to illustrate the qualities of leadership that won freedom in the men that "deliverit thair land all free," King Robert and his captains Edward Bruce, James Douglas, Thomas Randolph, and lesser men. It is a national and not simply monarchic and aristocratic war that he delineates. He refers approvingly to Scipio's manumission in an emergency of the Roman slaves, for free men fight best for freedom, and makes a renegade Scots noble tell the English king that Scotland is invincible because its farmers and ploughmen fight as well as do its knights. He has the distinctively Scottish attitude to kingship: his hero-king is concerned for more than his feudal rights, he grieves for his people, is at home with men of all classes, greets personally each man as he comes for the fighting at Bannockburn. An effect of the author's nationalism is a very human realism that seeks to "schaw the thing richt as it wes." Thus romantic fiction is eschewed, and, though such terms as "chivalry" and "courtesy" are used, the former refers to achievements in war, "birnand, slayand and distroyand," and the latter is applied to incidents such as the king's halting his little army so that a laundress can have her baby in safety. Language is appropriately sober and simple as befits Barbour's view of his nation, "the few folk of ane symple land," and in this kind has the truly heroic manner:

> His worschip and his mekill mycht
> Maid all that war with him so wicht
> That thai mycht neuir abaysit be
> Quhill forouth thame thai mycht him se.

The "mesure" that shows in his style, emotive only at grand points, appears also in his differentiation of character, Bruce's wisdom and Douglas's "sutelte" being regularly contrasted with the alleged impulsiveness of Edward Bruce and Randolph. It has been said that Barbour's *Bruce* is more chronicle than poem, but the shaping conception is always apparent, and when the reader reaches the approving sentence, "Thir lordis dyit apon this wyis," he has been made aware of a great action worthily interpreted.

—Matthew P. McDiarmid

BARCLAY, Alexander.   Scottish.   Born, probably in Scotland, c. 1475. May have studied at Oxford and Cambridge universities. Travelled in Italy and France; took holy orders; Chaplain, College of Ottery St. Mary, Devon, c. 1508–11; became a monk of the Benedictine monastery at Ely, 1511, and later of the Franciscan order at Canterbury; Vicar, Great Baddow, Essex, 1546–52; Rector, All Hallows, London, 1552. *Died 10 June 1552.*

PUBLICATIONS

Collections

The Ship of Fools (includes *The Mirror of Good Manners* and *Eclogues*), edited by Thomas H. Jamieson.   2 vols., 1874.

Verse

The Castle of Labour, from a work by Pierre Gringore.   1503; edited by A. W. Pollard, 1905.
The Ship of Fools of the World, from a work by Sebastian Brant.   1509.
The Life of Saint George.   1515; edited by William Nelson, 1955.
Eclogues 1–3.   1530; *Fourth Eclogue,* 1521; *Fifth Eclogue,* 1518; edited by Beatrice White, 1928.
The Mirror of Good Manners, from a work by Dominicus Mancinus.   1523.

Other

The Life of the Blessed Martyr Saint Thomas.   1520.
The Introductory to Write and to Pronounce French.   1521; selections edited by Alexander J. Ellis, in *On Early English Pronunciation,* 1871.
A Little Chronicle.   1525.

Translator, *The War Against Jugurtha,* by Sallust.   1520.

Bibliography: in *The Ship of Fools,* 1874.

Reading List: "Barclay: A Product of His Age" by S. Guttman, in *Papers of the Michigan Academy 35,* 1951; "Barclay and the Edwardian Reformation" by R. J. Lyall, in *Review of English Studies,* 1969.

*   *   *

To anyone expecting idyllic pastoral poetry in the tradition of Theocritus or Virgil the five *Eclogues* of Alexander Barclay must come as a decided shock. Instead of a golden world where shepherds, free from the curse of labour, can devote their time to love and song, we find a harsh, cruel rural environment, a land of storms, flood, bitter cold, hunger, and disease.

The shepherds, typical English rustics despite their conventional Italianate names, can only complain about their wretched plight and take refuge in the thought that, however intolerable these physical discomforts may be, the moral pollution of the court or town is even worse.

This is the excuse, in Eclogues I, II, and III, for a lengthy diatribe against the corruptions of the court, consisting mainly of a translation of the *De Curialium Miseriis* of Aeneas Sylvius – clumsy when literal, but vigorous and homely when Barclay adapts the Latin original to his English context or adds local references ("Bentleyes ale which chaseth well the bloud," IV, 722). The satirical targets in the final two eclogues are rich men and town-dwellers, and the source here is largely Mantuan.

For all the rural realism of the pastoral framework, it is clear that Barclay's main interest is in the satire: he is fascinated by the idea of the court as an "ymage infernall,/Without fayre paynted, within uggly and vile" (I, 1260–1). This discrepancy between appearance and reality extends to the inhabitants – "oft under yelowe lockes/Be hid foule scabbes and fearfull French pockes" (I, 358–9); but worst of all is the instability of courtly life, the need to flatter, the backbiting, the informing, the capriciousness of princes – "No love, no favour, fayth not fidelitie" (I, 1005). In the face of this, who would not prefer the philosophy of stoic endurance that keeps the shepherds morally unscathed in their rural solitude?

It is worth noting that Barclay's shepherds adhere to the principal of stylistic decorum laid down in the Preface: "it were not fitting a heard or man rurall/To speake in termes gay and rhetoricall" (Prologue, 83–4). And Cornix and Coridon do indeed have at their disposal a fund of rough, colloquial speech which they deploy with gusto in describing, for example, the nocturnal inconveniences of a communal sleeping-chamber at court: "Some fart, some flingeth, and other snort and route./Some boke, and some bable, some commeth dronke to bed...Some spue, and some pisse, not one of them is still" (III, 106–110). Local references, proverbs, and rustic similes ("nimis tepidum" becomes "hote as horse pis," II, 632) all demonstrate Barclay's concern to transform the rather bald Latin of his originals into something more closely approximating the homely diction of English shepherds.

This typical combination of crude native speech in the service of satire extends to Barclay's other major work, *The Ship of Fools*, a translation of Locher's Latin version of the *Narrenschiff* by Sebastian Brant. This remarkable poem surveys the entire spectrum of late Mediaeval society and casts a satirical eye upon an enormous variety of human failings: lascivious women, decayed clergymen, obsessed bibliomaniacs, corrupt lawyers, avaricious doctors – all have their place reserved aboard the Ship of Fools, and the overall picture is one of the whole world rushing headlong to destruction in the grip of wilful vanity, stupidity, and ignorance. The tone of this complaint is perhaps sterner than that of the Eclogues – the voice of the preacher is more obviously to the fore: "Thus is this Covetous wretche so blyndly led/ By the fend that here he lyveth wretchydly/And after his deth damned eternally" ("Of Avaryce," 19–21). Moreover, each section concludes with an explicitly didactic "envoy of Barklay to the Folys," usually recommending penance and self-control as a means of avoiding the "infernal pains" of hell.

But it is the vivid pictures of folly in action that remain with the reader: Barclay's homely vernacular can effortlessly bring to life characters such as the harlot, who "syttyth in the strete as past both shame and fere/Hir brestes bare to tempt them that pass by/Hir face anoyntyd blasynge abrode hir here" ("Of bodely pleasour," 15–17); or the victims of drunkenness, of whom "Some are Ape dronke full of lawghter and toyes/Some mery dronke syngynge with wynches and boyes/Some spue, some stacker some utterly ar lame ..." ("Of glotons," 111–113).

If *The Ship of Fools*, on account of its length and heavy didacticism, is unlikely to find much of an audience today, Barclay's *Eclogues* at least deserve our attention, not just because they represent the first set of eclogues written in English, but because in so many ways – their combination of pastoral and satirical elements, their adherence to stylistic decorum, their dry humour, their refusal to emulate the Arcadian escapism of the Continental eclogue – they anticipate a much greater work published more than sixty years later: it is impossible to determine whether Spenser actually read Barclay, but it is surely of considerable interest that the very qualities that have directed so much critical attention to *The Shepheardes Calender* are to be found in the humbler, less ambitious, but no less enjoyable *Eclogues* of Alexander Barclay.

—A. W. Lyle

———————

BEOWULF POET.

PUBLICATIONS

Verse

De Danorum Rebus Gestis Seculis III et IV Poema Danicum Dialecto Anglosaxonica, edited by Grim. Johnson Thorkelin.   1815.
Beowulf and the Fight at Finnsburg, edited by Fr. Klaeber.   1922; revised edition, 1950.
Beowulf and the Finnsburg Fragment, edited by C. L. Wrenn.   1953; revised edition, 1958.
Beowulf: A Verse Translation, by M. J. Alexander.   1973.

Reading List: *Beowulf: The Monsters and the Critics* by J. R. R. Tolkien, 1937; *The Audience of Beowulf* by Dorothy Whitelock, 1951; *The Art of Beowulf* by Arthur G. Brodeur, 1959; *Beowulf: An Introduction* by R. W. Chambers, revised by C. L. Wrenn, 1963; *The Structure of Beowulf* by Kenneth Sisam, 1965; *A Reading of Beowulf* by Edward B. Irving, 1968; *Beowulf and Its Analogues* by G. N. Garmonsway and J. Simpson, 1968.

*   *   *

The *Beowulf* poet is anonymous, but most scholars have placed him North of the Thames, in the Anglian kingdoms in the early or middle eighth century, and have supposed him to be a Christian nobleman or ecclesiastic, since the poem has some Christian and aristocratic colouring. The Northumbria of the Age of Bede (died 735) and the Mercia ruled by Offa from 757 to 796 have suggested themselves as the milieux where such a monumental court poem might have been composed and appreciated. The language of the poem supports such a provenance, though the Late West Saxon form in which it survives (in a unique manuscript of about the year 1000, now in the British Library) overlies the largely Anglian language of its composition.

We know less about the *Beowulf* poet than we do about Homer, since we lack even his (or her) name, but it is proper to think of a *Beowulf* poet rather than of the author of *Beowulf*, since the monster-slaying story and its associated historical material seem to have been in circulation long before the poem achieved its literary form of 3,182 Old English verses. The name of Beowulf the Geat does not appear elsewhere, but his king,. Hygelac, is recorded by Bishop Gregory of Tours as having died in a raid on the Franks in 521. The setting of the poem is Southern Scandinavian, and the historical and legendary characters, such as Offa the

Angle and Hrothgar the Dane, belong to the heroic Age of Migration, before the Angles had fully settled in Britain, a land which is not mentioned in the poem.

The *Beowulf* poet seems to have inherited not only his matter but also his medium of composition (and his world-view) from his Germanic ancestors. The language and style of *Beowulf* are shaped by the traditions of public, oral-formulaic verse composition, and recitations are described several times in the poem. Christianity and literacy, however, also contribute to *Beowulf*, which portrays a heroic world from a post-heroic and even elegiac viewpoint. The poem achieves a profound synthesis between these pre-Christian and Christian traditions, and its Anglian redactor may have been a "unifier" (a meaning of the Greek *Homēros*) as well as a creator.

The story of Beowulf, who slew monsters in his youth and a dragon in his last fight, is set in a world of heroic feuds between the tribes of the Baltic and North Seas. After his death his own people will be over-run by their neighbours; the seeds of the destruction of heroic civilisations are seen to be contained in the heroic code itself, where magnanimity and courage are accompanied by the duty of revenge. The monster Grendel and his mother, who terrorise the Danes, are the descendants of Cain, the first murderer; Tolkien interprets them as embodiments of evil. Human heroic society is portrayed in the ceremonious and hospitable court of Hrothgar at his hall, Heorot, where a poet sings of the creation of the world; Grendel attacks Heorot at night, and devours the bodies of the sleeping Danes: "Night's table-laughter turned to morning's/lamentation."

A young Geat, Beowulf, comes to Heorot to rid it of Grendel. Beowulf is an exemplary hero, loyal, generous, brave, courteous, and gentle, though of immense bear-like strength, and above the common motive of revenge. He heeds Hrothgar's warnings against pride and complacency in his youthful successes, but falls in old age against the dragon who ravages the Geat countryside after his hoard has been robbed of a golden cup. Some recent critics have developed Christian interpretations of the poem in which the hero is doomed by the limitations of his paganism; but the emphasis of the ending is clearly admiring:

> Then the warriors rode around the barrow,
> twelve of them in all, athelings' sons.
> They recited a dirge to declare their grief,
> spoke of the man, mourned their King.
> They praised his manhood and the prowess of his hands,
> they raised his name; it is right a man
> should be lavish in honouring his lord and friend,
> should love him in his heart when the leading-forth
> from the house of flesh befalls him at last.
> This was the manner of the mourning of the men of the Geats,
> sharers in the feast, at the fall of their lord:
> they said that he was of all the world's kings
> the gentlest of men, and the most gracious,
> the kindest to his people, the keenest for fame.

Beowulf is the longest Old English poem, and easily the most considerable piece of literature in English before the reign of Richard II. It has a grave and profound understanding of life and has poetic merits of the highest sort; it is a work of art of mature complexity and balance.

—M. J. Alexander

CHAUCER, Geoffrey.   English.   Born in London, c. 1343. Possibly educated at Oxford or Cambridge. Served in the King's forces in France, 1359; captured and ransomed, 1360. Married Philippa de Roet c. 1366; probably had two sons, one daughter. Entered the household of Lionel of Antwerp, son of King Edward III, as a page, 1357; on return from France entered the royal service under the patronage of John of Gaunt, 1360; promoted to Valet to Edward III, 1367, and Esquire, 1368; sent to Italy to assist in arranging a trade agreement with the Genoese, 1372, on diplomatic mission in France, 1377; Controller of the Customs and Subsidies on Wool, Port of London, 1374–86; Justice of the Peace, and Knight of the Shire (Member of Parliament) for the County of Kent, 1385–86; Clerk of the King's Works, 1389–91. Granted a pension, 1394. *Died 25 October 1400.*

PUBLICATIONS

Collections

Complete Works, edited by F. N. Robinson.   1933; revised edition, 1957.

Verse

The Parliament of Fowls, edited by W. Caxton.   1477; edited by D. S. Brewer, 1960.
Minor Poems, edited by W. Caxton.   2 vols., 1477.
The Canterbury Tales, edited by W. Caxton.   1478; edited by John M. Manly and
    Edith Rickert, 8 vols., 1940; edited by Nevill Coghill, 1972.
Troilus and Criseyde, edited by W. Caxton.   1484; edited by R. K. Root, 1926; Corpus
    Christi College, Cambridge, Manuscript, 1977.
The House of Fame, edited by W. Caxton.   1484.
The Book of the Duchess, in *Works.*   1526.
The Legend of Good Women, in *Works.*   1526.
The Romaunt of the Rose, in *Works.*   1532; edited by R. Sutherland, 1967.

Other

The Book of the Astrolabe, in *Works.*   1526; edited by R. T. Gunther, 1930.

Translator, *The Consolation of Philosophy,* by Boethius, edited by W. Caxton.   1478.

Bibliography: *A Bibliography of Chaucer* by A. S. Cook, 1886; *Five Hundred Years of Chaucer Criticism and Allusion* by C. F. E. Spurgeon, 3 vols., 1925; *Bibliography of Chaucer 1908–53* by D. D. Griffith, 1955, supplement by W. R. Crawford, 1967.

Reading List: *Chaucer and His Poetry* by George Lyman Kittredge, 1916; *The Poet Chaucer* by Nevill Coghill, 1947; *The Mind and Art of Chaucer* by J. S. P. Tatlock, 1950; *Chaucer* by D. S. Brewer, 1953, revised edition, 1973; *Of Sondry Folk: The Dramatic Principle in the Canterbury Tales* by R. M. Lumiansky, 1955; *A Reader's Guide to Chaucer* by Muriel Bowden, 1965; *Chaucer Life Records* edited by M. M. Crow and C. C. Olson, 1966; *Chaucer* by John Lawlor, 1968; *Chaucer: An Introduction* by S. S. Hussey, 1971; *Chaucer and the English Tradition* by Ian Robinson, 1961; *Chaucer and the Making of English Poetry* by P. K. Kean, 2 vols., 1972; *Chaucer's Dream Poems* by James Winny, 1973; *Chaucer* by John

Norton-Smith, 1974; *Chaucer: The Critical Heritage* edited by D. S. Brewer, 2 vols., 1976; *The Life and Times of Chaucer*, 1977, and *The Poetry of Chaucer*, 1977, both by John Gardner.

*   *   *

The appreciation of Geoffrey Chaucer has suffered a good deal in the past from his reputation as the "Father of English poetry." It has been easy to think of him as a "naif," the possessor of a charming simplicity of outlook which tends to convey itself, for a modern reader, through language considered "picturesque" or simply childish, alternately "quaint" or redolent of innocence for readers who think of themselves as more sophisticated and more psychologically complex.

All this is a long way from the truth about Chaucer, whose work is not so much the beginning as the fruit of a long development of civilization, and whose personality, as reflected in that work, is subtle, penetrating, and very deliberately elusive. His early poems show him engaged in exploring the possibilities of the English language as an instrument for sophisticated literary creation. The earliest poem of any length, *The Book of the Duchess* (1370), was almost certainly written as a eulogy for the recently dead Blanche, Duchess of Lancaster, in the form of a consolation addressed to her husband, John of Gaunt. Adapting the conventions of a love-vision to the purposes of an elegy it handles its theme with the exquisite tact which the delicate subject-matter must have required, and contrives in the process to reflect seriously, but without pretentious solemnity, on the natural grief to which bereavement gives rise, and on the need to temper that grief with a realistic acceptance of the humanly inevitable.

A second poem, *The House of Fame*, which must have been written some years later, was left conspicuously unfinished, as though Chaucer, having reached the moment of climax towards which he was moving, felt dissatisfied with the nature of his effort and impelled to make a fresh beginning. Before breaking off, he contrives to present himself in a typically self-depreciatory way and, in the process of reflecting on the nature and uncertainty of literary fame, to direct a good deal of unemphatic satire at the expense of his more serious poetic predecessors, including very notably Dante. Finally, in *The Parliament of Fowls* (c. 1380), Chaucer marries a dream-vision, based in part on Macrobius's version of Cicero's *Dream of Scipio*, to a vivid debate conducted by very human birds who have assembled before the goddess of Nature to choose their mates on St. Valentine's Day. The poem, which is perhaps the most finished of Chaucer's lesser writings, is marked by an exquisite blend of humour and seriousness; and, as in the other poems, much of its effect is obtained through the gently ironic presence of the narrator-poet, simultaneously involved in his creation and inviting on the part of the reader a saving detachment in its regard.

These early works led eventually, in *Troilus and Criseyde* (c. 1379–1383), to the first of Chaucer's two mature masterpieces: a long poem which clearly invites comparison, by its scope and universality, with the great Italian models – Dante, Petrarch, Boccaccio – which had by now in part replaced or supplemented the original French sources of his inspiration, and which he clearly thought of as capable of standing with the great poets of classical antiquity – "Virgil, Ovide, Omer, Lucan and Stace," as he lists them in bringing his poem to a conclusion – and of being incorporated as a work in the vernacular into the great tradition to which he asserted his right of entry.

Troilus and Criseyde is the first great poem to be written in what we can call "modern" English. Based principally on Boccaccio's treatment of the story in his *Filostrato*, Chaucer's poem shows him notably expanding his subject matter and, in the process, giving it an entirely new dimension. Boccaccio's is the story of two young lovers who conduct their relationship on lines laid down by the literary convention of courtly love and who are frustrated by the adverse external reality represented by the Trojan war. The tone is sophisticated, and on occasion cynical, and the author is evidently remembering, as he writes, his own vain attachment to the Napolitan lady Maria d'Aquino. Chaucer, by comparison, notably "medievalizes" his source and invites us, through his typically ambivalent narrator, both to participate in the unhappy story of love ending in betrayal and to see the events described in the light of a "philosophic" vision which sees disappointment and betrayal as the inevitable alternative face of "romantic" love. His pair of lovers, whom he treats with a marvellously sustained blend of detachment and sympathy, differs from those of Boccaccio in being notably young, inexperienced, and insecure, while the figure of the go-between, Pandarus, who plays a relatively minor role in the Italian story, is developed with a humour and psychological depth so far unparalleled in English literature. The result is a poem of superb and balanced humanity which, taking for a background the always relevant reality of the Trojan war, concentrates on the interlocking fortunes of three central personages, giving at each turn a new sense of depth to old conventions and inserting them into a narrative progress geared at each moment to the larger processes of a destinally conceived universe and conducted to its necessary conclusion through deceptively fluent, forward-moving verse.

If it can be argued that *Troilus and Criseyde* is Chaucer's most "artistic" and his most deliberately contrived poem, *The Canterbury Tales*, the writing of which occupied the last fifteen years of his life and remained unfinished at his death, constitutes unquestionably his greatest work. Aiming at the portrayal of a society, a "fellowship," on its various levels, it imparts to each of the individuals taking part in a journey, a pilgrimage to the shrine of St. Thomas Becket at Canterbury, a significance that emerges as more than merely personal (though it always remains certainly, and splendidly, all that is implied by *that*), to produce finally the effect of something like an allegory, a figural reflection of human life in time. As William Blake put it, over four hundred years later: "Of Chaucer's characters, as described in his Canterbury Tales, some of the names are altered by Time, but the Characters themselves for ever remain unaltered and consequently they are the Physiognomies or lineaments of Universal Human Life beyond which Nature never steps."

The Canterbury Tales is a series of stories told by an interacting group of characters in the course of a journey which is seen, in accordance with a common medieval conception, as an image of human life in time. The pilgrims travel from the Tabard Inn in Southwark to Canterbury, where they will recognize their sins and hear Mass at the shrine of "the holy blisful martir": but their journey is, beyond this, a "figure" for that of each and every man from birth to death, and in his quest for fulfilment in the "heavenly Jerusalem," outside and beyond the temporal process, which is his final and necessary goal. In the course of the journey the tales told by the pilgrims illuminate their respective natures and respond to significant facets of human life; and, as they move onwards, they are shown reacting to one another, more especially in the vivid interludes which constitute one of Chaucer's most significant contributions to his theme. Some of the interventions — more especially those of the Knight, the Wife of Bath, and the Pardoner — are so developed as to constitute nodal points around which it seems that the matter of the pilgrimage is largely concentrated; and beyond this, beyond the tales in their rich variety, we are aware throughout of a subtle distinction between the pilgrim-narrator, participating in the journey and responding with apparent naivety to much of what he sees, and the poet shaping his material from outside and lending to it his own detached, humorous, and barely definable irony. The final impression, as the journey draws to its close, is one of the necessity, and the limitation, of tale-telling in its relation to whatever "truth" men may be able to discern in the course of their common journey through life. The poet has given imaginative life to all his creatures — to the Miller not less than to the Knight whom he sets out to "quite," to the Pardoner not less than to the Parson, to the Wife of Bath not less than to the Clerk who tells the story of the "patient" Griselda. By so doing, and by refusing to reduce the complexity of life to an arid or impoverishing moralizing scheme, he has been true to the nature of his vocation as he has come to understand it in the course of a life-time devoted to the working out of its full implications. The same regard for "truth," however, impels him to recognize at the last that imaginative creation has its limits, and that what is, on its own terms, complete, valid, and satisfying is necessarily the *shadow*, the incomplete and partial reflection of a greater reality to which it points but which it cannot, in its time-conditioned and transient humanity, expect to compass.

Towards the end of *The Franklin's Tale*, Chaucer puts into the mouth of his central character the phrase "Trouthe is the hyeste thyng that man may kepe." The word "trouthe," indeed, in its medieval acceptance, which is considerably more ample than that generally associated with our modern "truth," seems to come closer than any other to conveying Chaucer's distinctive sense of human life. "Trouthe" is, in the first instance, the reality of things, which men at their peril ignore or seek to distort in the interest of their desire to live comfortably in the pursuit of illusion. As such it needs to be accepted in a spirit of "patience," by which Chaucer means not an attitude of supine or unnatural resignation, but rather a realistic acceptance of what is not subject to change or manipulation. But "trouthe" is also that "trust" by which men realize their *human* "truth": the trust which is based on an understanding of the "bond" by which they are drawn together and in recognition of which they fulfil their essential humanity. Finally, "trouthe" is also related to the word "betroth" and so with "marriage," in which the free and mutual gift of self becomes, for man, the central manifestation of the universal "bond" by recognizing which men and women incorporate themselves into the order of a universe conceived as a manifestation of creative, overflowing "love." In this cluster of related and mutually illuminating meanings concentrated on the rich connotations of a single word, we touch perhaps most closely the essential source of Chaucer's inspiration.

—Derek A. Traversi

CYNEWULF.   Anglo-Saxon; late 8th or 9th century.

PUBLICATIONS

Collections

The Poems, translated into English prose by Charles W. Kennedy.   1910.

Verse

Andreas und Elene, edited by J. Grimm.   1840; *Elene* edited by P. O. E. Gradon, 1958.
The Fates of the Apostles, in Appendix B to *Cooper's Report on Rymer's Foedera*, by B. Thorpe.   1869; *Andreas and The Fates of the Apostles* edited by Kenneth R. Brooks, 1961.
Christ, edited by I. Gollancz.   1892; *Christ: A Poem in Three Parts: The Advent, The Ascension, and The Last Judgment*, edited by Albert S. Cook, 1900.
Juliana, edited by W. Strunk.   1904; edited by Rosemary E. Woolf, 1955, revised edition, 1966.

Reading List: "Cynewulf and His Poetry" by Kenneth Sisam, in *Proceedings of the British Academy 18*, 1932; *Cynewulf and the Cynewulf Canon* by S. K. Das, 1942; *Critical Studies in the Cynewulf Group* by C. Schaar, 1949; "The Diction of the Signed Poems of Cynewulf" by R. E. Diamond, in *Philological Quarterly 38*, 1959.

*   *   *

Cynewulf is the author of four extant Old English poems, *Elene*, *The Fates of the Apostles*, *Juliana*, and the second of three poems which collectively are called *Christ*. The first two are found in the *Vercelli Book* and the others in the *Exeter Book*, both of around 1000 A.D., though the language of the poems suggests that they were composed in the ninth century somewhere in the Anglian area (i.e., north of the Thames). Cynewulf's authorship is known because he included in each of these poems autobiographical epilogues, in the texts of which he contrived to interweave his name in runic letters.

Juliana is a conventional saint's life, recounting the heroine's determined resistance to marriage with a powerful pagan nobleman. She suffers indescribable torture and dies a martyr's death. Cynewulf's lack of interest in straightforward narrative is shown by the long section in which the devil is made to confess to Juliana the evil deeds he has contrived since the world began. There are two large gaps, the result of missing leaves in the manuscript, but the lost passages can be reconstructed by reference to a Latin prose source.

The first part of *Christ B* is a dramatic treatment of the Ascension, and in the second and rather longer part Cynewulf adds his own comments, drawing upon a variety of sources ranging from patristic writings to vernacular gnomic verse. *Christ B* is separated in the manuscript from the other *Christ* poems, but there are no great differences in style and all of them could conceivably be the work of Cynewulf, although *B* alone contains his signature. The three events dealt with in the complete poem – Nativity, Ascension and Last Judgement – were often treated together in early Christian art.

In *The Fates of the Apostles* Cynewulf enumerates briefly the deeds and deaths of the twelve Apostles in a style reminiscent of the secular heroic poem *Widsith*. He mourns the passing of former glory in a reflective, elegiac mood which is found in other of his poems.

Elene is Cynewulf's masterpiece. It tells the story of the discovery and veneration of Christ's Cross by Saint Helena, mother of Constantine the Great. Beginning with an account of Constantine's conversion, it goes on to relate the mission of Helena and the refusal of the Jews to help. The Jewish spokesman, Judas, is made to suffer imprisonment and torture, and is eventually converted and leads the searchers to where the cross is buried, proving its authenticity by performing with it a miraculous cure. He assumes the new name of Cyriac, becomes a bishop, and later, with the aid of a miraculous light, discovers the Crucifixion nails. The poem ends with a reference to the Feast of the Elevation of the Cross, which was perhaps the occasion for which it was written. Cynewulf's source was a version of the Latin *Life of Saint Cyriac*, but he developed this in his own way, concentrating on the main events, using secular poetic diction for descriptions of battles, speeches, journeys, etc., and externalising emotional events (e.g., Judas's altercation with the devil at the time of his conversion). The passages describing the Cross have unmistakable parallels in the better-known poem *The Dream of the Rood*.

Most Old English poems are anonymous, the only other exceptions being Caedmon's *Hymn* and Bede's *Death Song*. Many others have at some time in the past been attributed to Cynewulf, but such theories do not find much support in the present day.

—G. A. Lester

DOUGLAS, Gavin. Scottish. Born at Tantallon Castle, 1474 or 1475; son of the third Earl of Angus. Educated at the University of St. Andrews, 1490–94; studied for the priesthood. Rector of Monymusk, 1496, of Glenquhom, 1498; Parson of East Linton and Rector of Prestonkirk, 1499; Provost of St. Giles, Edinburgh, 1501–14; Bishop of Kunkeld, 1515–20. *Died in September 1522.*

PUBLICATIONS

Collections

Poetical Works, edited by J. Small.   4 vols., 1874.
Douglas: A Selection from His Poetry, edited by Sydney Goodsir Smith.   1959.
Shorter Poems, edited by Priscilla Bawcutt.   1967.

Verse

The Palace of Honour.   1553(?).
The XII Books of Virgil's Aeneid Translated into Scottish Metre.   1553; edited by David F. C. Coldwell, 4 vols., 1957–64.

Reading List: *Douglas: A Critical Study* by Priscilla Bawcutt, 1976.

*   *   *

Of the only two significant works attributed with certainty to Gavin Douglas, *The Palice of Honour* and the great translation of Virgil, the first is of small value as literary art. *The Palice of Honour* is a long allegorical poem, traditionally medieval, about man's quest for honor, with elaborate mythological machinery and the typical fusion of Christian ideas with classical lore. The poem reveals immense scholarly learning, but is mediocre in style, often boring, with little to suggest the poetic power that was to emerge a dozen years later.

Douglas's fame, then, rests solidly upon his *Eneados,* a vigorous rendering in Middle Scots of the *Aeneid* of Virgil (12 books), together with the fifteenth-century sequel (Book XIII) by Mapheus Vegius, prefaced by thirteen original "prologues" by Douglas himself. Considered simply as a verse translation of Virgil this remains today, after nearly five centuries, among the finest in British literature. Indeed, Ezra Pound (in *How to Read*) goes so far as to argue that Douglas's version is poetically superior to Virgil's work itself! At any rate, it is a magnificent translation, based on sound principles. In the fascinating Prologue to Book I, Douglas explicitly states his aims: to produce a version that adheres faithfully to Virgil's text, while at the same time capturing something of the spirit and feeling of the original. The result is a fairly "free" translation; Douglas always renders Virgil's meaning with reasonable accuracy, but does not hesitate to add images of his own for greater clarity and vigor. Thus, on occasion, he will expand a single line of Virgil into two or even three.

In this task Douglas faced a formidable language problem, as he himself explains. He was, incidentally, the first to call his language "Scottis," as distinguished from "Inglys" or "sudron," and he recognized that his mother tongue was often inadequate for purposes of classical translation. Accordingly, like earlier Scots poets, he felt free to coin or to Scotticize scores of Latinate words to suit his special needs. In this way he achieved a rich and flexible amalgam, combining the dignity and precision of Latinate terms with the colloquial strength of his Scots.

Douglas's "prologues" are in themselves a remarkable creative achievement, ranging through a wide gamut of subject matters and styles – from literary criticism (Prol. I) to religious and moral preachments (Prols. IV, VIII, XI) to powerful nature poetry (Prols. VII, XII, XIII), from the high style to the earthy. In these wholly original prefaces, Douglas shows extraordinary poetic talent, especially in the great "nature" prologues in which he presents amazingly detailed and compelling pictures of the various seasons in Scotland.

Altogether, the *Eneados*, with its entrancing new prologues and its splendidly strong and colorful rendering of old Virgil, is one of the major performances in Scots poetry.

—Allan H. MacLaine

DUNBAR, William.   Scottish.   Born in East Lothian, c. 1460. Educated at the University of St. Andrews, 1475–79, B.A. 1477, M.A. 1479. Joined the Franciscan order, and for a time was a begging friar, later left the order; subsequently served James IV as both court poet and diplomatic envoy until 1513; granted court pension, 1500–13. *Died c. 1522.*

PUBLICATIONS

Collections

Poems, edited by D. Laing.   2 vols., 1834; supplement, 1865.
Poems, edited by J. Small.   3 vols., 1884–93.
Poems, edited by W. Mackay Mackenzie.   1932; revised edition, 1960.
Selected Poems, edited by Hugh MacDiarmid.   1955.
Poems, edited by James Kinsley.   1958.

Reading List: *Dunbar: The Poet and His Period* by R. A. Taylor, 1932; *Dunbar: A Biographical Study* by John W. Baxter, 1952; *Dunbar: A Critical Exposition of the Poems* by Thomas M. Scott, 1966; *Two Scots Chaucerians* (Dunbar and Henryson) by H. Harvey Wood, 1967.

*   *   *

William Dunbar, the greatest of the Scottish Makars (or Scottish Chaucerians, as they are sometimes referred to by the English), and one of Scotland's three finest poets (the others being Burns and MacDiarmid), was not only a man of moods, of extreme exultations and dejections which are reflected in his work, but a virtuoso deploying his brilliant technique upon several styles, all of them – whether the aureate, the vernacular, the secular, or the religious – shot through with contrasted lights, and characterised by energetic brush-strokes. For these reasons, even Dunbar's use of the mediaeval literary man's stock-in-trade phrases, like *A per se, fyre on flint, hair like golden wire* stand out more sharply than in the gentler context of Henryson's poetry.

We know a certain amount about Dunbar's life from official sources, but much more about his nature and manner of living from his personal poems. The dampness and draughtiness and the long, dark hours of a Scottish winter depressed him, as he tells us in "On His Heid-Ache":

> Whone that the nicht dois lengthen hours,
> With wind, with hail and heavy schours,
>   My dule spreit does lurk for schoir,
>   My hairt for langour does forloir.
>
> For laik of simmer with his flours.
> I walk, I turn, sleep may I nocht,
>   I vexit am with heavy thocht ...

Yet he was well aware of the subjective nature of his depression, and made an effort to master it, concluding "Ane His Awin Enemy" with an exhortation:

> Now all this time lat us be mirry,
> And set nocht by this warld a chirry,
>   Now, whill thair is gude wine to sell,
> He that does on dry bread wirry,
>   I gif him to the Devil of hell.

Although he held minor orders in the church, the Christian affirmation in his roll-call of dead poets in "Lament for the Makaris," with its liturgical use of the tolling refrain *Timor mortis conturbat me*, is scarcely enthusiastic:

> Sen for the deid remeid is none,
> Best is that we for dede dispone,
> Eftir our deid that lif may we:
>   *Timor mortis conturbat me.*

As a fluent exponent of the Scots tradition of "flyting" – hurling versified abuse at your opponent without regard either to good manners or accuracy – he achieved resounding effect in "The Flyting of Dunbar and Kennedy." His sharp, satirical muse found comic exercise in unfrocking the pretensions of John Damien to fly, using birds' wings, in "The Fenyeit Freir of Tungland." "The Treatis of the Twa Maryit Wemen and the Wedo," in which the three ladies discuss what interests them most, their sex lives, shows Dunbar as a master of comedy, a role in which he appears more delightfully in "The Ballad of Kynd Kittock." (Although no manuscript of this associates it with Dunbar directly, there could scarcely have been another undiscovered master-poet capable of writing it in Dunbar's style alive at the same time.)

In full aureate flight, Dunbar's great Christmas and Easter hymns ring out like solemnly triumphant organ-music. Here is the sonorous opening of " Of the Resurrection of Christ":

> Done is a battle on the dragon black,
> Our campioun Christ confoundet hes his force;
> The yetts* of Hell are broken with a crack,   *gates
> The sign triumphal rasit is of the croce,
> The divillis trymmillis with hiddous voce,
> The sauls are borrowit and to the bliss can go,
> Christ with his blud our ransonis dois indoce:
> *Surrexit Dominus de sepulchro.*

He could turn off a set of begging verses, seeking a benefice for himself from the King, with a skill which made them outlive the occasion that called them forth. He produced a mellifluous flourish for Margaret Tudor when she arrived in Scotland for her marriage to James IV in 1503:

> Now fair, fairest, of every fair,
> Princess most pleasant and preclare,*   *famous
> The lustiest* one alive that been,   *most beautiful
> Welcome of Scotland to be Queen!

Indeed, he seems to have remained a favourite with the Queen, travelling to Aberdeen with her in 1511, and saluting that city with an aureate splendour he matched in another poem on London.

"The Dance of the Seven Deidly Sins," characterised by rhyming exuberance and remarkable verbal energy, the anti-Highland "Epetaffe for Donald Owre," its sharp short lines stabbing home the poet's angry contempt, and his splendid love-allegory "The Golden Targe," full of the colours of leaves and flowers, and birdsong newly refreshed by sunshine after rain, further reveal the breadth of Dunbar's forceful genius. MacDiarmid, in his best work, outdid him in intellectual range as Burns outdid both of them in his warmth of human concern. But out of the mediaeval shadows, Dunbar, cavorting in the Queen's chamber, celebrating the main religious festivals of his church or setting down aspects of his daily life, displays a commanding personality, a skill with vocabulary and a competent mastery of stanza-forms nowhere surpassed in Scottish literature.

—Maurice Lindsay

GAWAIN POET.

PUBLICATIONS

Collections

Manuscript edited by I. Gollancz.   1923.
Complete Works of the Gawain Poet in a Modern English Version by John Gardner.   1965.
Works, edited by Charles Moorman.   1976.
Pearl, Patience, Cleanness, and Sir Gawain and the Green Knight, edited by A. C. Cawley and J. J. Anderson.   1976.

Verse

Sir Gawain and the Green Knight, edited by J. R. R. Tolkien and E. V. Gordon.   1925; revised by Norman Davis, 1967; edited by R. A. Waldron, 1970.
Pearl, edited by E. V. Gordon.   1953.
Patience, edited J. J. Anderson.   1969.
Cleanness, edited by J. J. Anderson.   1977.

Reading List: *Sir Gawain and Pearl: Critical Essays* edited by Robert J. Blanch, 1966; *The Pearl-Poet* by Charles Moorman, 1968; *The Gawain-Poet: A Critical Study* by A. C. Spearing, 1970; *The Gawain-Poet* by Edward Wilson, 1977; *The Art of the Gawain-Poet* by W. A. Davenport, 1978.

*   *   *

The Gawain-Poet is the name usually given to the unknown author of *Sir Gawain and the Green Knight* and, by implication, of the three other poems, *Pearl, Patience* and *Cleanness* (sometimes called *Purity*), which appear with *Gawain* in the unique manuscript, British Library MS Cotton Nero A.X. The attribution of all four poems to the same poet (also called the Pearl-poet, *Pearl* being the first poem in the manuscript) is now generally accepted, if only for the sake of convenience. The strongest arguments for common authority are the striking parallels of theme, imagery, and style between the four poems. *St. Erkenwald*, which survives in a different manuscript, has often been attached to the group as a fifth poem from the same pen, but the evidence is not strong.

The four poems of Cotton Nero A.X. are the crowning achievement of the "Alliterative Revival" of the fourteenth century. This resurgence of writing in the traditional unrhymed alliterative measure has never been satisfactorily explained as a historical phenomenon, but it can certainly be associated primarily with the west and north-west of England, and perhaps with the noble households of that region. The language of the *Gawain*-poems has been localised in the region where Lancashire, Cheshire, and Derbyshire meet, and the composition of the poems has been ascribed to the last quarter of the fourteenth century. *Patience* and *Cleanness* are in the traditional form of the alliterative long line, while in *Gawain* the lines are grouped into "stanzas" of variable length (101 in all) by the insertion of five short rhymed lines ("the bob and wheel") at the end of groups of unrhymed long lines. *Pearl* is not written in the alliterative long line, but in complex 12-line stanzas (again 101 in all) based on a line of more conventional metrical (i.e. syllabic) form with heavy and regular alliteration.

Patience and *Cleanness* are cast in the form of homily based on biblical story: both recommend a virtue by portraying how God treats its opposite. In the former, the story of Jonah, through which the poet displays God's imperturbable patience contrasted with man's childish petulance and bad temper, offers full play to the poet's brilliant dramatic gifts. The human comedy of Jonah's evasions is exploited without prejudice to any of the story's moral and typological significance, while the language of dramatic realisation combines an unforgettable quality of visual imagination with an unrelaxing didactic purpose. No-one can forget the image of Jonah entering the whale's jaws "as mote in at a minster-door," but the image serves as a reminder too that Jonah's three-day sojourn in the whale's belly was a figure of Christ's entombment and therefore of the potentiality of resurrection. *Cleanness* is a longer, more loosely constructed poem, and illustrates God's punishment of three kinds of uncleanness – sexual promiscuity, sodomy, and sacrilege – in the stories of the Flood, the destruction of Sodom, and the fall of Belshazzar. Other biblical stories provide insets to these main narratives. The portrayal of God's anger often releases a fierce and terrifying power of imagination, but the remorseless moral certainty of the poem is fascinatingly combined with a cool and quizzical humanity which will for instance see the victims of God's wrath in touchingly human contexts ("Love looks to love, and his leave takes," as the Flood advances) or detect even a note of wryness in God's voice.

Pearl takes the form of a vision, in which the dreamer, lamenting the loss of his "pearl" (an infant daughter), is transported to a heavenly landscape where, across the river of death, he sees his daughter. She, now a Bride of Christ in the Heavenly City, instructs him in the ethics of grief and salvation. The dreamer's grief and bewilderment at his loss are treated with some poignancy, but the poet's main purpose is to show the nothingness of worldly concerns in the light of a transcendental understanding. To do this, he first draws us into the dreamer's grief and makes us emotionally aware of the need for solace, and then proceeds to show how every worldly attachment of the dreamer, every "natural" human expectation, must be transformed if true understanding is to be attained. The transformation is effected through delicate play with the fiction of a "dramatic" relationship between the dreamer and the Pearl-maiden (rather as with Dante and Beatrice), and perhaps most brilliantly through the metamorphosis of the pearl-image itself, from mutable object to very symbol of bridehood and communion with the Lamb. Every word and image in the poem, every speech and passage of description, is part of a consummate design to bring a transcendental and ultimately incommunicable truth within reach of the imagination.

Sir Gawain and the Green Knight differs from the other three poems in that it is not overtly didactic. It is a romance, and, on one level, quite simply the best romance that was ever written. It has a brave and noble hero, a fierce and mysterious other-worldly antagonist, a seductive temptress, and throughout an incomparable rendering of the splendour and gaiety of courtly life. Gawain braves all dangers, resists all temptations, and in the end returns to Arthur's court, the challenge of the Green Knight met and overcome. Yet a kind of ironic comedy flickers about the whole story, and the plot – in which Gawain fulfils the first public challenge, that of the beheading game, only to discover that his performance is to be assessed on the basis of another challenge, that of the bedroom temptations, which he thought was private – is a marvellous structure for reducing the paragon of romance-heroes to an almost comically bewildered state of self-justification and self-accusation. He has done all that a man could be expected to do, but he knows he should have done more. What is a romance-hero for, if not to attain the unattainable? In these scenes, the poet seems to be writing a sophisticated critique of romance, and to be questioning the possibility of a high secular idealism which combines chivalric with Christian values. Yet he does so, as always, without contempt, generous in a measured way towards man in his predicament and rich in his response to the vigour and beauty of life.

—Derek Pearsall

GOWER, John.   English.   Born in London, c. 1330. Married Agnes Groundolf in 1397. Possibly travelled in France in his early life; after returning to England settled down to life as a country gentleman; also in the service of Henry of Lancaster, later Henry IV. A friend of Chaucer. Went blind c. 1400. *Died in 1408.*

PUBLICATIONS

Collections

Complete Works, edited by G. C. Macaulay.   4 vols., 1899–1902.
Major Latin Works (translated into English), edited by Eric W. Stockton.   1962.
Selections, edited by J. A. W. Bennett.   1968.

Verse

Confessio Amantis.   1483; selections edited by R. A. Peck, 1968.
Vox Clamantis (in Latin), edited by H. O. Coxe.   1850; in *Major Latin Works,* 1962.
Chronica Tripartita and Minor Poems (in Latin), edited by H. O. Coxe.   1850; in *Major Latin Works,* 1962.
Mirour de l'Omme, in *Complete Works.*   1899–1902.

Reading List: *Studien zu Gower* by M. Wickert, 1953; *Gower: Moral Philosopher and Friend of Chaucer* by John H. Fisher, 1964; *Gower: Dichter einer Ethisch-Politischen Reformation,* 1965, and *Gower: Zur Literarischen Form Seiner Dichtung,* 1966, both by Edwart Weber; *Love, The Word, and Mercury: A Reading of Gower's Confessio Amantis* by Patrick J. Gallacher, 1975.

*   *   *

Chaucer addresses John Gower as "moral Gower" in the dedication of *Troilus and Criseyde,* and probably Gower would have found the epithet neither inapt nor unappealing. His earliest poetic works were a lengthy moral treatise in Anglo-Norman (then the standard literary language of polite society) called the *Mirour de l'Omme,* and a violent diatribe in Latin on the ills of contemporary society, the *Vox Clamantis.* In the late 1380's, however, perhaps emboldened by Chaucer's example, Gower began the long poem in English on which his reputation mainly rests, the *Confessio Amantis,* and the *Confessio* is something more than a moral poem.

It begins with a long Prologue, in which Gower analyses once again, in a familiar vein, the corruption in English society. But he turns then, more lightly, to themes of love, the ubiquitous and all-consuming interest of courtly literature, and promises to write "somewhat of lust, somewhat of lore." The frame of the narrative is the Lover's Confession, in which, as in a penitential manual, the Lover (*Amans*) confesses his sins against Love to Genius, the Priest of Venus, and, after listening to strings of exemplary stories relating to each of the Seven Deadly Sins (133 in all, constituting something over half the total 33,444 lines of the poem), receives absolution. The stage seems set for the charmingly immoral morality of the "religion of love," but it soon becomes clear that Gower is using love, because of its intrinsic interest and because it is the area where man's moral being is most under challenge, as the point of reference for a scheme of traditional and rational morality. His view of love is a proper, decent and sensible one, and virtuous love is for him the control of passion, the intrinsic "goodness" of which he nowhere denies, through the exercise of reason. Thus a "sin" against love is likely to be a sin by any definition and not a paradoxical virtue.

Gower's treatment of the frame narrative is both witty and poignant, full of dry and rueful comedy in which the Lover "hops alway behind," and ending with a strangely moving epilogue in which the Lover, aged and impotent, is pensioned off from the service of Venus. There is much delightful play here with the *persona* of the Lover and his relationship to the poet. The great strength of the *Confessio,* however, is in the inset narratives, where Gower shows himself to be a narrative poet of warm human sensitivity and compassionate understanding. He takes the stories far beyond their prescriptive or exemplary function into a world where virtuous conduct is seen to spring from fineness and unconstrained decency of feeling, rather than obedience to law, and can therefore seek out a consistent universe of moral value even in stories so barbaric as those of Tereus and Medea. It is the stories of women betrayed or deceived in love that call forth his readiest imaginative sympathy, and he has a power of communicating positively the worth of the love lost as well as the sadness of its loss. Whatever role as keeper of the nation's conscience he may have cast himself for, Gower understood truly in his poetry the "civilisation of the heart."

—Derek Pearsall

HARY (Blind Harry or Hary; Henry The Minstrel). Scottish. Probably a native of Lothian, born c. 1440. Nothing is known of his life except his blindness, his occupation, and that he probably served in the Scottish court of James IV, 1490–92. *Died c. 1495.*

PUBLICATIONS

Verse

Hary's Wallace, edited by Matthew P. McDiarmid. 2 vols., 1968–69.

Reading List: *The Wallace and the Bruce Restudied* by J. T. T. Brown, 1900; "On Blind Hary's *Wallace*" by George Neilson, in *Essays and Studies 1*, 1910; *Mythical Bards and the Life of William Wallace* by W. H. Schofield, 1920; "William Wallace and His 'Buke' " by W. Scheps, in *Studies in Scottish Literature 6*, 1969.

*   *   *

The nationalism that had inspired Barbour's *Bruce* is more fiercely articulate in Hary's *Wallace*, not only because fifteenth-century writing tends to be more emotive than fourteenth-century but also because the poem is polemical. It is aimed against James III's novel and dangerous policy of preferring an English to a French alliance. It implicitly supports those rebellious nobles who were soon to depose the king and accuse him of "the inbringing of Englishmen," and rebukes the "thrifty men" whose commercial interests made them willing to forget the lessons of the Wars of Independence. It is to impress these lessons that Hary presents Wallace as an example of unrelenting patriotism, a martyr sold to the enemy by selfish and disloyal fellow countrymen.

History happens to support this representation, but, unlike Barbour, Hary is more concerned to make history than to record it: lays and traditions are rehandled, episodes are imitated from the *Bruce*, a time-scale that will allow him to treat this extended matter in twelve Books is devised, and actions and scenes are invented, all in order to develop a hero whose sufferings are greater even than his achievements. Loss of father, brother, wife, friends, office (as Guardian of Scotland), life itself, and an unappreciated loyalty to king and country, are so presented as to make Wallace the tragic victim of an unnatural world

(" 'Allace,' he said, 'the warld is contrar-lik!,' " XI, 210). The Wallace who so deeply affected the imaginations of "Ossian," Burns, and Wordsworth is Hary's creation, a figure larger than life who anticipates the protagonists of sixteenth-century drama in the intensity of his responses and the passion of his purpose. Pity for his, and his country's, wrongs is both modified and heightened by the shock of an unremitting, if principled, vengefulness. No historical personage had been so emotively presented, nor scenes of violent action (guerilla warfare) so effectively visualised. The poet's vision, however, so intense in parts – the episodes of the killing of Fawdon, "The Barns of Ayr," at Falkirk the betrayal of Wallace along with his winning Bruce for the cause – is felt to be finally obsessive and tiring. The driving pace of his narrative dispenses with any subtleties of versification or interpretation. One remembers Wordsworth's verdict on Walter Scott that his genius was "physical." Hary is rightly called by Friedrich Brie "a heroically minded man" (in *Die Nationale Literatur Schottlands*, 1973), and it is as a heroic poet that he wins respect, for simple lines such as this on Wallace after the defeat at Falkirk, "Amang the dede men sekand the worthiest."

—Matthew P. McDiarmid

HAWES, Stephen. English. Born, probably in Suffolk, c. 1475. Educated at Oxford University. Travelled on the Continent after leaving university; returned to England and served at court: groom of the chamber to Henry VII, from c. 1502. *Died c. 1523.*

PUBLICATIONS

Verse

The Pastime of Pleasure. 1509; as The History of the Grande Amour, 1554; edited by
    W. E. Mead, 1927.
The Conversion of Swearers. 1509.
A Joyful Meditation to All England of the Coronation of King Henry the Eighth. 1509.
The Example of Virtue. 1509(?).
The Comfort of Lovers. 1515(?).
The Minor Poems (all but The Pastime of Pleasure), edited by Florence W. Gluck and
    Alice B. Morgan. 1974.

Reading List: *Hawes Passetyme of Pleasure Vergleichen mit Spensers Faerie Queene* by F. Zander, 1905; "The English Chaucerians" by Derek Pearsall, in *Chaucer and Chaucerians* edited by D. S. Brewer, 1966.

*   *   *

In an age more richly endowed with poets of undisputed quality than the early sixteenth century, the verse of Stephen Hawes might appear to be merely of minor interest, yet such were the problems and uncertainties concerning metre, language, form, and content which confronted Tudor writers that the striking historical importance of his work outweighs its technical shortcomings. Hawes is a typical early English Renaissance author, still remaining conservative in literary taste and outlook, yet attempting to breathe life into outdated medieval conventions. Despite its inadequacies, his poetry retains the fascination of a transitional mode where modern topics and concerns struggle to detach themselves from earlier literary preoccupations which obscure their potential novelty and prevent their full expression. Never a conscious pioneer, if he chiefly looks back to post-Chaucerian moral allegory and chivalric romance for his models, Hawes also glances ahead to the theme and methods of *The Faerie Queene*.

His poems, the principal of which is the lengthy *Passetyme of Pleasure* dedicated to his master Henry VII, exemplify the officially sanctioned voice of early Tudor poetry, and exhibit the formal "high" style of which Hawes was an earnest and untiring exponent; the lyric grace of the song-books, the colloquial gusto of Skelton, the subtle rhythms of Wyatt, are nowhere to be found. He writes in the approved "aureate" manner of his poetic mentor John Lydgate at his most ornately periphrastic, "tellynge the tale in termes eloquent" in order to conceal the presumed crudities of the native vernacular, but his command of language is often uncertain, his epithets banal, his imagery rarely arresting. He seems to adhere to no firm metrical principles, even unorthodox ones, and his grammar and syntax can often leave a reader at a loss to discover the poet's intended meaning.

Yet from Hawes's structurally weak, conscientiously embellished, and imaginatively pedestrian verse emerges a man responsive to his literary heritage, natural and formal beauty, the chivalric ideal, and the traditional wonders and marvels of the knightly quest. *The Passetyme of Pleasure* depicts human life as an allegorical pilgrimage and devotes almost 6,000 lines to Graunde Amour's valiant efforts to win the hand of La Bell Pucell by performing feats of arms against a variety of enemies, strengthened by coaching received in the Tower of Doctrine from the Seven Liberal Arts, and assailed by the misogynistic (and somewhat wearisome) attacks of a loutish dwarf, Godfrey Gobelyve. Here Spenser is undoubtedly foreshadowed, and *The Example of Vertu*, in which Youth is guided through numerous temptations by Discretion to slay a three-headed dragon, marry Cleaness, daughter of the King of Love, and depart for a dwelling in Heaven, anticipates the adventures of both the Red Cross Knight and Sir Guyon. Hawes's tribute to Henry VIII is a standard Renaissance eulogy, and his versified sermon, *The Convercyon of Swerers*, is unlikely to appeal today, but *The Conforte of Lovers*, which describes an allegorical dream-vision culminating in an amorous encounter in a garden setting, is not without charm or merit.

—William M. Tydeman

HENRYSON, Robert.   Scottish.   Born in Scotland c. 1425. The facts of his life are mainly conjecture: possibly educated abroad; Master of Arts; a clergyman; held a clerical appointment within Dunfermline Abbey; Headmaster of the abbey grammar school; practised as a notary from 1448. Possibly an original Member of the University of Glasgow, 1462. *Died c. 1506.*

PUBLICATIONS

Collections

> *Poems*, edited by G. Gregory Smith.   3 vols., 1905–09.
> *Poems*, edited by H. Harvey Wood.   1958.
> *Poems*, edited by Charles Elliott.   1963; revised edition, 1974.

Verse

> *The Testament of Cresseid*, in *Works*, by Geoffrey Chaucer.   1532.
> *The Moral Fables of Aesop the Phrygian in Eloquent and Ornate Scottish Metre*.   1570.

Reading List: *Five Poems* by E. M. W. Tillyard, 1948; *Henryson* by Marshall W. Stearns, 1949; *Henryson: A Study of the Major Narrative Poems* by John MacQueen, 1967; *Two Scots Chaucerians* by H. Harvey Wood, 1967.

*   *   *

Robert Henryson is a poet of the highest stature, the full extent of whose individuality and artistry has perhaps only been established comparatively recently. But his profound human sympathies, his keen sense of humour, his narrative skills, and his gift for characterisation have always assured him the affection and respect of readers willing to overcome the minor difficulty presented by his language. What has been recovered by the work of recent critics is something approaching the fuller medieval dimension of his work. In its turn this has enhanced our appreciation of his creative individuality, of the serious moral complexion of his work, and of his craftsmanship.

To assert Henryson's individuality is to raise a common issue with regard to medieval literature – its reliance upon commonplaces, conventions, and traditions. The old term – "Scottish Chaucerian" – applied to him and the other great Scottish poets of the period similarly implies indebtedness, lack of originality, and imitation. There can be no doubt of Chaucer's influence upon him; his use of the Chaucerian "rhyme royal" and the enlargement of Chaucer's *Troilus and Criseyde* are the most conspicuous instances. Neither is there any question of the extent to which Henryson worked consciously within the wider European context, drawing both widely and in some detail upon the full range of the literary tradition from learned scholasticism to the more popular Aesop and the beast epic of Reynard the Fox. But he shows himself equally a poet determined to stamp all with his own mark. "Quha wait if all that Chaucer wrait was true."

The Testament of Cresseid is the single poem of Henryson's which has received the greatest attention and the highest praise. In part its popularity has been due to its association with Chaucer's great narrative, to which it provides a kind of sequel, following as it does the "fatall destinie/Of fair Cresseid, that endit wretchitlie." But the conception of her tragic end appears to be entirely Henryson's own. The narrative proper begins with a laconic passage characteristic of the tragic tone of the poem:

> Quhen Diomeid had all his appetyte,
> And mair, fulfillit of this fair ladie,
> Upon ane other he set his haill delyte
> And send to hir ane Lybell of repudie,
> And hir excludit fra his companie.

Desolate, she curses the gods for having deceived her, and provokes a dream sequence in which she is summoned before the assembled gods and condemned for blasphemy. The punishment imposed upon her is leprosy. Begging with "cop and clapper," she joins the band of disfigured outcasts in the leper house, until the day that Troilus, fresh from success in battle, comes riding past on his return to Troy. This final meeting of the lovers is the more tragic and moving because they fail to recognise one another, although something in her appearance brings Cresseid into his mind, and prompts him to pour riches into her lap before riding on his way. When she discovers the identity of the knight who "hes done to us so greit humanitie" she acknowledges for the first time her own guilt and faithlessness, makes her testament, and dies repentant. "Nane but myself as now I will accuse."

In view of the harshness of her tragic fate, and the movement of Cresseid from infidelity to distress, to blasphemy, to humiliation and misery, and then to repentance, it is worth stressing the way Henryson avoids the pitfall of sententious moralising and ensures that the final effect is indeed tragic, and not something cruder. This is, of course, a matter of tone. The displacement by which punishment is exacted for blasphemy (rather than for her infidelity and the suggestion of promiscuity) helps achieve it. The moral climate she inhabits is subject to swift reversals and powerful ironies. The gods who preside are untrustworthy, like Venus, or malevolent, like Saturn. Henryson on occasion deliberately withholds moral judgement, and maintains throughout a sympathy for Cresseid which is genuine and sincere, for her fall could hardly have been more absolute. Her epitaph measures its depth:

> Lo, fair laydis, Crisseid, of Troyis toun,
> Sumtyme countit the flour of Womanheid,
> Under this stane lait Lipper lyis deid.

In terms of imaginative texture too the poem is rich. Her leprosy, for example, is linked with the attributes of astrological-mythological gods who judge her, and carries also the suggestion of venereal disease as the punishment of her lust and prostitution. As her triumphs were of the flesh, so is her terrible punishment. And this complex of images is associated with another which begins in the winter blast that opens the poem, which is woven through the poem in the references to Cresseid as flower and in the wintry portrait of Saturn, and which makes its last appearance in her epitaph.

The thirteen *Moral Fables* Henryson retails derive from the European traditions of Aesop and the Reynard cycle. They vary considerably in form and function: some are more or less developed as narratives than others; some are highly political and satirical of social abuse; others restrict themselves to allegorical interpretations of a moral or theological nature. All, however, consist of a narrative followed by a moralitas, and in all cases the moralitas (whatever else it may convey) carries a Christian allegory. The Christian allegory is the profoundest level at which the stories function, and provides an absolute standard against which the other levels of moral comment are to be related. When such comment appears to accord ill with the values implied in the narrative, or to represent some kind of tour de force of interpretation, it is safer to regard them as amplifications of the number of ways in which the stories may be read, rather than excluding one reading in favour of another. One consequence is the range of Henryson's *Fables*, stretching through religious, theological, moral, social and political dimensions. And there is very fruitful interplay between the medieval Christian view of human affairs on the one hand, and the concern with this world Henryson exhibits, whether through celebration or satire. A perspective emerges here from which both gain.

The medieval Christian commonplace prevails elsewhere in his shorter works, such as "The Abbey Walk," "The Three Deid Pollis," and "The Prais of Age." But much of the expression of Christian scorn of the world comes in the form of dissatisfaction with the way the broadly political dispensation of the world operates. This is so consistent in Henryson it can only in part be attributed to conventions of *contemptu mundi*. The tensions between Henryson's vital celebrations of natural and human and his ultimate Christianity are articulated explicitly and implicitly, in, for example, "The Reasoning Between Youth and Age" and fables like "The Preiching of the Swallow." It is in this that his attractive humanism consists.

—Brian W. M. Scobie

HEYWOOD, John. English. Born, possibly in North Mimms, Hertfordshire, c. 1497. Educated at Oxford University. Married Eliza Rastell in the 1520's; two sons, including the writer Jasper Heywood. Associated with the court of Henry VIII, and with Sir Thomas More and his circle: court musician and music teacher to Princess Mary, from whom he afterwards received a pension; received court payments in 1519 and 1520 as a singer; admitted to the liberties of the City of London, 1523; Steward of the King's Chamber, later Queen's Chamber, 1528–58; involved in a plot to overthrow Cranmer, imprisoned and pardoned, 1544; left England for religious reasons in 1564, and lived in Belgium until his death. *Died in 1578.*

PUBLICATIONS

Collections

  Dramatic Writings, edited by J. S. Farmer.   1905.
  Works, and Miscellaneous Short Poems, edited by B. A. Milligan.   1956.

Plays

  John John, Tib, and Sir John.   1533; edited by J. S. Farmer, in *Two Tudor Shrew Plays,* 1908.
  The Pardoner and the Friar.   1533; edited by J. S. Farmer, 1906.
  A Play of Love.   1533; edited by K. W. Cameron, 1944.
  The Play of the Weather.   1533; edited by K. W. Cameron, 1944.
  The Four P's.   1543(?); edited by F. S. Boas, in *Five Pre-Shakespearean Comedies,* 1934.
  Witty and Witless, edited by F. W. Fairholt.   1846; edited by K. W. Cameron, 1941.

Verse

  A Dialogue Containing All the Proverbs in the English Tongue.   1546; revised edition, 1561; edited by R. E. Habenicht, 1963.
  An Hundred Epigrams.   1550; later editions add 500 more.
  A Ballad Specifying the Marriage Between Our Sovereign Lord and Lady.   1554.
  The Spider and the Fly.   1556; edited by A. W. Ward, 1894.
  A Ballad Touching the Taking of Scarborough Castle.   1557.

A Ballad Against Slander and Detraction.   1562.
Works.   1562.
Of a Number of Rats.   1562 (?).

Reading List: *The Life and Works of Heywood* by R. W. Bolwell, 1921; "Heywood and His Friends" and "The Canon of Heywood's Plays," in *Early Tudor Drama* by A. W. Reed, 1926; *Heywood, Entertainer* by Rupert de la Bère, 1937; *French Farce and Heywood* by Ian C. M. Maxwell, 1946; *Heywood* by Robert Carl Johnson, 1970.

*   *   *

John Heywood is the best-known exponent of the Tudor interlude. The canon of his work has never been established, but he certainly wrote *Witty and Witless, A Play of Love, The Play of the Weather, The Four P's,* and probably also *John John, Tib and Sir John* and *The Pardoner and the Friar.*

Tudor interludes were secular dramatic entertainments performed mainly at banquets in private houses and at court. Short plays were therefore appropriate, and none of Heywood's is longer than about 1,500 lines. Because of the environment in which they were performed, there is a sense of intimacy and audience contact, particularly in *The Play of the Weather* in which the antics of the "Vice," Merry Report, resemble those of the Elizabethan Fool.

Thin in plot, Heywood's interludes sometimes come closer to debate than drama. *The Four P's,* for example, introduces a contrast between a Palmer, Pardoner, 'Pothecary, and Pedlar as to who can tell the best lie. In *The Play of the Weather* the characters lodge successive pleas to Jupiter to send the Weather which suits them best. *Witty and Witless* (the weakest and perhaps the earliest of Heywood's surviving plays) presents three characters debating ponderously the relative merits of ignorance and wisdom. *The Pardoner and the Friar* has some rudimentary dramatic action in that the characters eventually come to blows over the merits of their respective professions. But the real exception is *John John, Tib and Sir John,* which is modelled on a French farce. It presents the typical *fabliau* triangle of jealous husband, amorous wife, and priestly lover, and makes clever use of double entendre, the priest enjoying the wife's "pie" while the husband ineffectually tries to stop up a hole in a bucket with a piece of wax.

The plays are, in themselves, poor "theatre," being composed mainly in monotonous couplets, with entrances and exits unskillfully managed, but there is supplementary material in the form of songs, which reflect Heywood's interest in music as master of the royal choir school. Children probably acted alongside adults, and in *The Play of the Weather* there seems to be an awareness of the effective contrast between the adult characters and the boy,"the least [i.e., smallest] that can play," who comes to request a plentiful supply of snow for snowballing.

The characters mostly represent distinct social types, like Lover-Not-Loved and Loved-Not-Loving who debate their relative unhappiness in *A Play of Love.* Heywood plagiarises the Prologue to Chaucer's *Pardoner's Tale* to provide an arresting beginning for his *The Pardoner and the Friar,* but the play rapidly deteriorates after this, and only in *John John* are the characters convincingly individualised.

Even the dullest of Heywood's interludes is not without its humour, though in all of them except *John John* it is of a verbal type which does not usually appeal to modern taste. Ribald antifeminism is common, and there is a strong element of frankly sexual innuendo.

Heywood was associated with Sir Thomas More and his circle, and suffered for his adherence to Catholicism. But concern with politics and moral issues is not noticeable in his work. However, his criticism of the abuses of the church, such as the activities of pardoners, is as vehement as Chaucer's. *The Play of the Weather,* perhaps the most successful of the plays, exposes society's self-interest and factionalism and there is nice irony in the fact that at the end everyone is deliriously happy to accept the varied weathers they are already receiving.

Heywood's abuse of women can be traced in his collection of 300 proverbs on marriage. He composed 600 epigrams, most of them lacking in pith, a verse parable called *The Spider and the Fly*, and a small number of ballads.

—G. A. Lester

HOCCLEVE, Thomas.   English.   Born, possibly in Hockcliffe, Bedfordshire, c. 1368. Appointed clerk in the Privy Seal Office, London, c. 1386, and held this position for 30 years. Granted an annuity by Henry IV, 1399. *Died c. 1430.*

PUBLICATIONS

Collections

Works (Regiment of Princes and Minor Poems), edited by F. J. Furnivall and I. Gollancz.   3 vols., 1892–1925; *Minor Poems* revised by Jerome Mitchell and A. I. Doyle, 1970.

Verse

Poems, edited by G. Mason.   1796.
De Regimine Principum, edited by T. Wright.   1860.

Reading List: *Six Medieval Men and Women* by H. S. Bennett, 1955; *Hoccleve: A Study in Early 15th-Century English Poetic* by Jerome Mitchell, 1968 (includes bibliography); "Conclusions: Hoccleve" by Penelope B. R. Doob, in *Nebuchadnezzar's Children: Conventions of Madness in Middle English Literature,* 1974.

*   *   *

The personal element in Thomas Hoccleve and his connection with Chaucer have engaged the attention of his readers over the years. A clear portrait of the poet emerges from his four principal "autobiographical" poems: *La Male Regle*, the Prologue to the *Regement of Princes*, the *Complaint* (in which he discusses his bout with insanity), and the *Dialogue with a Friend*. If the portrait is not flattering in all instances, it is certainly very human. Few Middle English poems contain passages of self-revelation comparable to those of Hoccleve in realism, individuality, and apparent sincerity; but even here the element of literary convention cannot be dismissed altogether.

Despite Hoccleve's assertion that he was a friend and pupil of Chaucer, it is doubtful that there was ever a close personal friendship between the two poets. The autobiographical significance of his often quoted lines in praise of Chaucer (in the *Regement of Princes*) has been exaggerated. The lines seem heartfelt because he utilized poetic conventions more convincingly than did his contemporaries in similar eulogies. The amount of his indebtedness to Chaucer for diction and phraseology has also been exaggerated. His name comes up frequently in connection with the famous portrait of Chaucer in the *Regement of Princes* (British Museum MS Harley 4866, fol. 88); this has been reproduced photographically in numerous places and is considered the finest and most authentic of all the Chaucer portraits.

Hoccleve was very much a man of his age. Literary taste in the fifteenth century is clearly reflected in his courtly poetry (e.g., the *Letter of Cupid*), his political poems (e.g., the *Address to Sir John Oldcastle*), his *De Regimine Principum*, his short begging poems, his religious verse (e.g., the *Mother of God*, formerly attributed to Chaucer), and his narrative poems (e.g., the *Tale of Jereslaus' Wife* and the *Tale of Jonathas*, translated from the Anglo-Latin *Gesta Romanorum*). He was not an innovator in his treatment of popular themes and in his handling of accepted genres; yet in small ways he often managed to give his work a distinctive character. In addition, he was a pioneer in introducing several well-known genres into English, such as the *Ars Moriendi* (i.e. his *Lerne to Dye*), the satirical panegyric of one's lady, and the manual of instruction for a prince. There is no truth in the often repeated allegation that he lacked metrical skill; his verse is *not* marred by "thwarted stress." His poetic technique is best understood and appreciated in the context of other medieval literature. Like Lydgate and other 15th-century poets, he looked on poetry as versified rhetoric, he used word pairs frequently, and he treated his sources freely. His strength as a craftsman can best be observed in passages of direct discourse, which are skillfully wrought in general and often remarkably lifelike in comparison with the French or Latin originals.

—Jerome Mitchell

HOLLAND, Sir Richard.   Scottish.   Born in Orkney, c. 1420. Had benefices in Orkney and in Caithness, Ross, and Moray, 1441–67: Vicar of Ronaldsay, Orkney, before 1467; Precentor, Elgin Cathedral Church; Notary for the Countess of Douglas, 1455. Went into exile in England with the Earl of Douglas, 1480.

PUBLICATIONS

Verse

Buke of the Howlat, edited by Frances J. Amours, in *Scottish Alliterative Poems,* vols. 1–2.   1892–97.

Reading List: *Hollands Buke of the Howlate* by Arthur Diebler, 1893; "Holland's *Buke of the Howlat:* An Interpretation by Matthew P. McDiarmid, in *Medium Aevum 38,* 1969.

*   *   *

Sir Richard Holland's *Buke of the Howlat* is a response – none appears in English poetry of the period – to the revolutionary ferment of Europe, the strife of nobles and clerics against the centralising absolutism of princes and popes. The Douglases felt threatened by royal policy, and in Church politics were leaders of the Conciliarist ("parliamentary" Church) party in Scotland. The young poet, however, is not polemical, though he praises the Douglas tradition, and the papal arms that he describes are those of the anti-pope elected by the Council of Basle, Felix V (1440–49). It is not the strife that inspires him but the familial harmony dreamt by a reformist Europe. Nature's God-given order, in which each nation, rank, and estate is to earn its happy place by selfless service to the community, is his theme. Understanding this, Walter Scott's denial of any serious and unifying concept can at last be dismissed and appreciation can begin. The basic fable is that of the unteachable Caliban-type owl, who protests the injustice of his wretched appearance and outcast's mode of life to a Council convened by the Pope and Emperor of birds, which duly submits the complaint to Dame Nature. She bids each species give one feather, and, when a second Council complains of the now splendid owl's tyrannical behaviour, explains, "My first making was unamendable." The protesting Howlat is man unfit for a Christian society, because without humility ("We cum pure, we gang pure, baith king and commoun").

Holland's lesson is enforced in a series of vivid scenes: an earthly paradise painted in the fresh colours of a May morning in Moray, where are "Mendis and medicyne for all mennis neidis"; European Councils, of which the Douglases are shown to be worthy members, where Church and laity "gang in a gait [unity]/Tendir and trew" and all is homely and festal harmony; the Howlat lonely again and self-upbraiding; the ideal lastly focussed in an image of the poet's married patrons as doves in the forest "tendir and tryde." Certainly there are moments of prolixity (the Douglas example makes a disproportionate if memorable effect), but the theme of a naturally happy society and as natural misfit is powerfully, sometimes beautifully, developed. The *Buke* shares with Chaucer's *Parlement of Foules* a debt to Alain de L'Isle's *De Planctu Naturae* but makes a more modern and meaningful use of it.

—Matthew P. McDiarmid

JAMES I, King of Scotland.   Scottish.   Born in Dunfermline, July 1394; son of Robert III. After capture by English, 1406, spent youth in detention; education supervised by Henry IV and by royal tutors, 1409–13. Married Lady Jane Beaufort, daughter of the Earl of Somerset, 1424 (died, 1445); one son, six daughters. Released from prison and repatriated, 1423; crowned King of Scotland, at Scone, 1424, and tried to restore divided and demoralized kingdom: his reforms in curtailing the powers of the Scottish nobles eventually provoked a conspiracy against him; he was murdered at Perth by assassins led by his kinsman Sir Robert Graham. *Died 20 February 1437.*

PUBLICATIONS

Verse

The Kingis Quair, edited by W. W. Skeat.   2 vols., 1911; edited by J. Norton-Smith, 1971; edited by Matthew P. McDiarmid, 1973.

Reading List: *James I, King of Scots* by E. W. M. Balfour-Melville, 1936; "Tradition and the Interpretation of The Kingis Quair" by John MacQueen, in *Review of English Studies*, 1961; "Chaucerian Synthesis: The Art of the Kingis Quair" by W. Scheps, in *Studies in Scottish Literature 8*, 1971; "A King's Quire" by J. A. W. Bennett, in *Poetica*, May 1976.

*   *   *

The genius of James I lies in his skill in blending Chaucerian and Lydgatian elements into a charming and harmonious exploration of personal experience, observation of nature, religious and philosophical insight, and dream adventure. Felicitous Chaucerian elegance of phrasing, reminiscence, and charm of thought intertwine with Lydgate's early penchant for a medley type of narrative construction where Chaucer's more sophisticated philosophical tendencies are lent a relaxed, "amateurish" formal shape. An acute philosophical awareness still informs the heart of the poem – James understands his Boethius better than many of his modern expositors – but it is a symptom of a modern distrust of "literature" which strives to strip the work of its marvellous variousness of appeal and genuine "gentle" charm of expression in order to promote metaphysical dilemmas and resolutions.

The poet's dream fascinates in its vividness, variety, and rapidity of movement. His vision comes after a long day's anxiety and offers answers to the poet's yearnings (recalling Chaucer's *Parlement*). It includes a lightning ascent through the spheres and almost Dantean meetings with divine personages. It contains a description of an ideal landscape populated by "diuerse kynd of bestes" (recalling the *Parlement*'s diverse kinds of birds). The dream is introduced dramatically by supernatural light and voice darting in through the window which offered the prisoner his only glimpse of the world from which he was barred – and through that window comes later the message of his *larges*. Finally, the poet-prince celebrates his "hertes hele," secure in an optimistic universe where Boethian perspectives invite us to admire the harmonizing justice of the poet's passage through exile and prison to liberation in true love. Or so it seemed in February 1424.

—J. Norton-Smith

LANGLAND, William. English. Born c. 1332. Educated, according to tradition, at the school of the Benedictine monastery at Great Malvern, Worcestershire. Clerk in minor orders; later moved to London. *Died c. 1400.*

PUBLICATIONS

Collections

Piers the Plowman, translated by J. F. Goodridge. 1959.
Selections (from the C-Text), edited by Elizabeth Salter and Derek Pearsall. 1967.
Piers Plowman: The B-Text: Prologue and Passus I-VII, edited by J. A. W. Bennett. 1972.

Verse

Piers Plowman:
A-Text: edited by George Kane, in *Piers Plowman: The A Version.* 1960.
B-Text: edited by George Kane and E. Talbot Donaldson, in *Piers Plowman: The B Version.* 1975.
C-Text: edited (with A-Text and B-Text) by W. W. Skeat. 1886; edited by Derek Pearsall, 1978.

Bibliography: "Piers Plowman: An Annotated Bibliography for 1900–1968" by Katherine Proppe, in *Comitatus,* 1972.

Reading List: *Piers Plowman: The C-Text and Its Poet* by E. Talbot Donaldson, 1949; *Piers Plowman and the Scheme for Salvation* by R. W. Frank, 1957; *Piers Plowman: An Introduction* by Elizabeth Salter, 1962; *Piers Plowman: An Essay in Criticism* by John Lawlor, 1962; *Piers Plowman as a Fourteenth Century Apocalypse* by M. W. Bloomfield, 1963; *Piers Plowman: The Evidence for Authorship* by George Kane, 1965; *Style and Symbolism in Piers Plowman* edited by Robert J. Blanch, 1969; *Piers Plowman: Critical Approaches* edited by S. S. Hussey, 1969; *Piers Plowman and Christian Allegory* by David Aers, 1975.

*   *   *

The poem generally called *Piers Plowman* exists in three versions, known as the A, B, and C versions, and all are now usually attributed to William Langland, of whom nothing is known but what is contained in some notes on his origin in a fifteenth-century manuscript and what can be deduced from his references to the dreamer, the "I" of his poem. From these, it appears that he was a cleric in minor orders who, his education half-completed, took up residence in London and there eked out a living saying prayers for hire and performing other odd ecclesiastical offices. The A-text, written in the 1360's, is a vision of the corruption of English society through the influence of money and self-interest, and of the attempted reform of that society through the agency of Piers Plowman, the representative of simple, honest Christian virtue and hard work. The failure of this attempt at social reformation in the first part of the poem (the *Visio*) prompts a turning inward, a search for the good life in the reformation of the will of the individual, in the second part (the *Vita de Dowel*), but this search is frustrated and incomplete. In the B-text, written in the 1370's, Langland revises the *Visio* extensively and then resumes the search of the *Vita*, making additions which altogether treble the length of the poem (to over 7,000 lines) and which bring the search, after many vagaries of will and understanding, to a triumphant conclusion in the vision of Christ as a transcendental Piers Plowman. The poem ends with a return to the disordered world of the fourteenth century and a vision of impending destruction. The C-text, probably left incomplete at Langland's death, is a piecemeal revision of all except the last two *passus* of B, with some ruthless jettisoning of what an older man saw as superfluities and some sharpening of the line of thought.

Langland chose a poetic form, the alliterative long line, which had long associations with homiletic and didactic writing, but used it in a free and informal, often prosaic manner completely different from that of the poets of the "Alliterative Revival," such as the *Gawain*-poet. He has few of their mannerisms of diction, syntax, and phraseology, and little consciousness of an alliterative *ars poetica*. His style has its own kinds of energy and particularity, but he is above all a missionary, a prophet, a voice crying in the wilderness, and niceties of language as well as versification give way to the urgency of communicating his vision.

That vision is of England and the life of the individual Christian corrupted and deformed through the influence of money. Langland sees the harmony of the estates, of a world structured in contractual obligation and mutual service, perverted to the remorseless ethic of money which dissolves all bonds of nature between man and man. He sees the Church as an institution devoted to the protection of its wealth and the extension of its privileges, its whole purpose of pastoral care, witness, and intercession blunted or forgotten. In the van he sees the friars, who have prostituted the office of confession and the sacrament of penance for the sake of profit, and who thus pervert the fundamental ministry of the Church and instead sow damnation. To combat this, Langland attempts to initiate nothing less than an immense revolution in the moral and spiritual life of society and the individual. He is part here of a larger movement which was sweeping Europe, and which responded to the growing isolation and rigidity of the Church by seeking a more personal kind of religion and a ministry closer to the original apostolic ideal.

Langland uses no set procedure for the communication of his vision. The first part of the poem, the *Visio*, is mainly an allegorical narrative of what the dreamer sees; the second part, the *Vita*, is mainly an allegorical narrative of what the dreamer experiences in his search for Dowel, the true Christian life, though he reverts to observer for the final visions of the Crucifixion, the Harrowing of Hell, and the coming of Antichrist. Within these broad structural patterns, a bewildering variety of allegorical and homiletic procedures are employed, with often only the enigmatic figure of Piers Plowman to beckon the dreamer on. Yet the poem has a profound unity, growing as it does out of a deep and prolonged search on the poet's own part for spiritual illumination and certainty. The activity of the poet's mind is embodied in the person of the dreamer who is both himself and not himself, and who engages the reader in the experience of the poem, so that its urgencies are shared, its discoveries seen and felt to be won. The representation of the progress of the dreamer to understanding is one of the poem's great sources of power, since it enforces participation rather than mere acquiescence.

Langland's other outstanding quality as a religious poet is the intense actualising power of his imagination, which annexes the world of experience and literal reality to the world of revelation and spiritual reality and makes them one. His great allegorical scenes, as of the Field Full of Folk, the Ploughing of the Half-Acre, or the Coming of Antichrist, are both intensely and memorably real, with a reality that tends to subsume all other ways of conceiving of his subject, and also receptive to a rich and wide range of allegorical significances. So too with the great moments of spiritual illumination in the dreamer's search for truth, like the Feast of Patience, or the meeting with the Good Samaritan: allegory here seems the only and perfect means through which the timeless and the temporal can be shown to intersect. This power of the concretizing imagination operates also in the detailed verbal texture of the poem where spiritual vision absorbs, sanctifies and is sanctified by a world of homely objects, most magnificently perhaps where Langland describes the origin in God's love of the Incarnation (B.I. 151–6). Here the spiritual world is made concrete, and the everyday world is spiritualised, in a vision truly made flesh.

—Derek Pearsall

LAYAMON.   English.   Born c. 1200.   Priest of Areley Kings in Worcestershire.

PUBLICATIONS

Collections

   Selections, edited by J. Hall.   1924.
   Selections, edited by G. L. Brook.   1963.

Verse

   Layamon's Brut, edited by Sir Frederic Madden.   3 vols., 1847.
   Layamon: Brut, edited by G. L. Brook and R. F. Leslie.   2 vols., 1963–78.

Reading List: *Layamon: An Attempt at Vindication* by G. J. Visser, 1935; *The Layamon Texts: A Linguistical Investigation* by N. H. P. Bøgholm, 1944; *Layamons Brut: Eine Literarische Studie* by H. Pilch, 1960.

*   *   *

All that is known of Layamon is what he tells us is in the prologue to his sole surviving work, the *Brut* (properly *Hystoria Brutorum* – the short title is taken from later popular histories): his name (the modern form of which is a conventionally accepted misspelling), and the fact that he was parish priest at Areley Kings, in Worcestershire. His poem, probably composed about 1225, survives in two manuscripts of the third quarter of the thirteenth century, both in the Cotton collection of the British Library (Caligula A.ix and Otho C.xiii). It is a metrical composite, using indiscriminately both a form of the Old English alliterative line without rhyme and short syllabic couplets of three or four stresses, and also various combinations of the two. Layamon seems consciously to have been adapting the native verse-traditions to Anglo-Norman (French) models.

   The *Brut* begins with Brutus, the eponymous founder of Britain, leaving Troy, and traces the history of Britain up to the death of Cadwallader, the last "British" king with serious claims to dominion in England. The basis for the story is Geoffrey of Monmouth's *Historia Regum Britanniae* (1130–38), one of the most influential books ever written, since it is the primary source for Arthurian legend, as well as the only source for stories of pre-Arthurian kings such as Lear and Cymbeline. Geoffrey took something from traditional legends, but invented more, his purpose being to supply Britain with the history it lacked, in the sober form of a Latin prose chronicle; to claim descent, along with Rome and other nations of Western Europe, from Troy; and to create a great national hero in Arthur. Geoffrey's work was translated into Anglo-Norman (French) verse by Wace, probably for the court of Henry II, with more dramatisation of the events of the story, more dialogue and a more "courtly" flavour. Wace was the direct source of Layamon, who seems not to have known Geoffrey.

   Layamon works back from Wace towards a more heroic and martial treatment of the story. His work on the first half of the poem is not memorable, but he comes into his own with the first appearance of Arthur at line 19,252. Arthur is a focus for all Layamon's imaginative energies, a figure who provides the opportunity for an expression of all his patriotic passions and all his love of heroic battle-poetry. In the Arthurian sections of the poem, Wace is a mere springboard for Layamon, who elaborates and amplifies the narrative here with unprecedented freedom. The battles of Arthur against the Saxon invaders led by

Childric are described with immense panache, with vigorous scenes of individual combat and mêlée punctuated by vows of vengeance, cries of denunciation and execration, paeans of scorn and triumph. Layamon introduces here, and only here, the epic similes for which he is famous, of Arthur as a wolf descending upon the enemy from the woods hung with snow (20120–25), or of the fleeing Saxons drowned in the Avon as "steelen fishes," their gold-bedecked shields glinting like scales (21319–28). If battles are the essence of heroic poetry, then Layamon is our greatest epic poet, and the *Brut* the only true national epic.

—Derek Pearsall

LYDGATE, John. English. Born in Lydgate, near Newmarket, Suffolk, c. 1370. Admitted to the Benedictine monastery at Bury St. Edmunds, Suffolk, 1385; ordained deacon, 1393, priest, 1397; studied at Gloucester College, Oxford, before 1408. Lived most of his early life in London; a friend of Thomas Chaucer; acted as court poet, and enjoyed the patronage of the Duke of Gloucester, from 1422; also wrote pageants and occasional verse for the Corporation of London; Prior of Hatfield Broadoak, Essex, 1423–34; returned to the monastery at Bury, 1434, and remained there for the rest of his life. Granted royal pension, 1423. *Died in 1449.*

PUBLICATIONS

Collections

A Selection from the Minor Poems, edited J. O. Halliwell.   1840.
Minor Poems, edited by H. N. McCracken.   2 vols., 1911–34.
Poems, edited by J. Norton-Smith.   1966.

Verse

The Horse, The Goose, and the Sheep.   1477; in Minor Poems, 1934.
The Churl and the Bird.   1477(?); in Minor Poems, 1934.
The Temple of Glass.   1477(?); in Poems, 1966.
The Life of Our Lady.   1484; edited by J. A. Lauritis and others, in Duquesne Studies, Philological Series, 1961.
The Fall of Princes.   1494; edited by Henry Bergen, 4 vols., 1924–27.
The Siege of Thebes.   1495(?); edited by Axel Erdmann and Eilert Ekwall,   2 vols., 1911–30.
The Interpretation of the Names of Gods and Goddesses.   1498; as The Assembly of Gods, edited by F. J. H. Jenkinson, 1906.
The Complaint of a Lover's Life.   N.d.; in Poems, 1966.
The Virtue of the Mass.   N.d.; in Minor Poems, 1911.

The Governance of King's and Princes.   1511; edited by T. Prosiegel, 1903.

The History, Siege, and Destruction of Troy.   1513; edited by Henry Bergen, 4 vols., 1906–35.

The Testament of John Lydgate.   1515(?); in *Minor Poems*, 1911.

The Proverbs of Lydgate.   1515(?).

Flower of Courtesy, in *Works of Chaucer*, edited by T. Thynne.   1532; in *Minor Poems*, 1934.

The Life of Saint Alban and the Life of Saint Amphabel.   1534; edited by J. E. van der Westhuizen, 1974.

The Danse Macabre, in *The Fall of Princes.*   1554; edited by F. Warren and B. White, 1931.

The Serpent of Division.   1559; edited by H. N. McCracken, 1911.

The Pilgrimage of the Life of Man, edited by F. J. Furnivall.   3 vols., 1899–1904; edited by Furnivall and Katharine Locock, 1905.

Two Nightingale Poems, edited by O. Glauning.   1900.

Reason and Sensuality, edited by E. Sieper.   2 vols., 1901–03.

The Grateful Dead, edited by A. Beatty, in *A New Ploughman's Tale.*   1902.

Reading List: *Lydgate: A Study in the Culture of the 15th Century* by W. F. Schirmer, translated by A. E. Keep, 1961; *The Poetry of Lydgate* by Alain Renoir, 1967; *Lydgate* by Derek Pearsall, 1970.

*   *   *

John Lydgate was probably born when Chaucer was in his mid-twenties. He was admitted to Bury St. Edmunds Abbey and remained attached to the foundation for the whole of his life, but for most of his life he lived outside the cloister. Lydgate had many important friends and "patrons": Henry V; Humphrey of Gloucester; Edmund Lacy, Bishop of Exeter; Isabell, Countess of Warwick; Thomas Montachute, Earl of Salisbury; Henry VI; John Whethamstede, Abbot of St. Albans. He knew nearly everybody, including Lord Mayors of London, Aldermen, and officials of the Royal Household. His special friends were the Chaucers of Ewelme, Thomas and Maud and their daughter Alice. He lived to a great age and his later works show the effect of fatigue and bad eye-sight (he complained of these). He should not be judged by the monumental hack-work he undertook as an historian and cultural cicerone (*Troy Book, Fall of Princes, Pilgrimage of the Life of Man, Life of Our Lady*).

The Bury monk's earlier poetry (before 1412) displays an interest in Chaucer's dream poems but simplifying Chaucer's poetic intelligence and urbane command of style and form. Yet *The Complaynt of a Loveres Lyfe* and *The Temple of Glas*, though emphatically didactic and matter-of-fact, are serious and interesting compositions. Autobiography enters in 1412 with the commission by the Prince of Wales of the *Troy Book*. The style cultivated by Lydgate for that work is assiduously based on Chaucer's Monk's art of versification. Later, when Lydgate undertook the *Life of Our Lady*, he assumed the learned naive style of Chaucer's *Life of St. Cecile*. This "functionalism" permits the poet a number of "styles," and those appropriated for an English Liturgical Style (aureation) and the neo-classical Latinate pressed into service for "A Defence of Holy Church" (1413–14) show Lydgate at his most inventive and eloquent. He seems never to have possessed the force of personality to cultivate this capacity for elegant, economical utterance. Lydgate's imagination was not a powerful shaping force. It is enfeebled by a too mechanical application of rhetorical discipline. His modest, shorter poems, "The Letter of Humphrey," the "Letter to Thomas Chaucer on his Departure for France," the beautiful "moral religious ballade" "As a Midsomer Rose," show his attractive, often delicate appreciation of sentiment, morality, and eloquence.

—J. Norton-Smith

LYNDSAY, Sir David.   Scottish.   Born in Cupar, Garmylton, near Haddington, c. 1490.
Educated at the University of St. Andrews. Married Janet Douglas in 1522. Courtier of James
IV: "usher" of the infant James V, 1512; employed on various missions to the Emperor
Charles V, and to Denmark, France and England; Lyon King-of-Arms, 1538. Knighted,
1542. *Died in 1555.*

PUBLICATIONS

Collections

   Poetical Works, edited by Douglas Hamer.   4 vols., 1931–36.
   Poems, edited by Maurice Lindsay.   1948.

Verse

   The Complaint and Testament of a Popinjay.   1538.
   *A Dialogue Betwixt Experience and a Courtier of the Miserable Estate of the
      World.*   1554; augmented edition, 1558.
   The Works.   1568.
   The History of a Noble and Wailzeaned Squire, William Meldrum.   1594; edited by
      James Kinsley, 1959.
   A Supplication in Contemplation of Side Tails and Muzzled Faces.   1690.

Play

   A Satire of the Three Estates, in Commendation of Virtue and Vituperation of Vice
      (produced 1540).   1602; edited by James Kinsley, 1954.

Bibliography: in *Poetical Works,* 1931–36.

Reading List: *Lyndesays Monarche und die Chronica Carionis* by A. Lange, 1904; *Lindsay* by
William Murison, 1938; *Dramatic Allegory: Lindsay's "Satyre of the Thrie Estaitis"* by
Joanne S. Kantrowitz, 1974.

*   *   *

Sir David Lyndsay differs from most of the other Scottish Makars in that much of his work
had a socio-political purpose. Appropriately, this led him to indulge less frequently in the "hie
style," although "The Deploratioun of Quene Magdalene," in *rime royal,* shows that he could
produce aureate word-music when formal royal occasion demanded. More typical, however,
is "The Complaynt of Sir David Lyndsay," in octosyllabic rhyming couplets, which reminds
James V of the poet's services since that time when

>   as ane chapman bears his pack,
>   I bore thy Grace upon my back,
>   And sumtynes, stridlings on my neck,
>   Dansand with mony bend and beck ...

and warns of the need for reform in the church. Lyndsay was a commonsense moderate, who urged the king to behave in a seemly manner in "The Answer to the Kingis Flyting," particularly in sexual matters. His most entertaining poems are *The Historie of ane Nobil and Vailzeand Squyer, William Meldrum*, a racy tale in two parts, "The Testament" in the Chaucerian heptastich, the rest in vigorous octosyllabic couplets; and, in the same metre, his attack upon woman's fashion, *Ane Supplicatioun Directed to the King's Grace in Contemplatioun of Syde Taillis*, a satire, however, which verges on becoming anti-feminist. "The Complaint of Bagsche, An Auld Hound," in octosyllabics, rhyming ababbcbc, is a further moral sermon, but suggests a possible prototype for Burns's "The Twa Dogs."

Lyndsay, indeed, set the conversational tone which was to be taken up and sharpened by the poets of the 18th-Century Revival. His masterpiece, the verse-morality play *Ane Pleasant Satyre of the Thrie Estatis*, presents a wide range of good and bad characters, the good embodying symbolically the obvious virtues desirable in Church and State, the bad, a much more witty and appealing gallery of contemporary rogues. The purpose of the play, which in places employs what was to become the 18th century's "Standard Habbie" stanza, was to urge the king to reform the Catholic Church. First staged in 1540, it failed in its purpose, and ten years later the Reformation swept the old faith aside. But the merits of the play survived the occasion that called it forth, and, shortened and slightly modernised, it has been several times revived with outstanding success at the Edinburgh Festival. It seems improbable that *The Thrie Estates* was Lyndsay's only play, and, indeed, he lays claim to others in *The Complaynt and Testament of the Papyngo* (Parrot), but these have not survived.

The most "modern" of the Makars in the directness of his human concern, and an enshriner of proverbial wisdom in easily remembered lines, Lyndsay enjoyed wide popularity, his work being found with the Bible in many a humble Scottish household until he was displaced from popular affection by Burns.

—Maurice Lindsay

MALORY, Sir Thomas.   Identification of the author is not certain: English; lived in the 15th century; from the late 19th century claimed by some scholars to be Sir Thomas Malory of Newbold Revell – a claim now disputed.

PUBLICATIONS

Prose

Le Morte Darthur Reduced into English.   1485; edited by Eugène Vinaver, 3 vols., 1947; revised edition, 1967.

Reading List: *Malory* by M. C. Bradbrook, 1958; *Essays on Malory* edited by J. A. W. Bennett, 1963; *Malory's Originality* by R. M. Lumiansky, 1964; *The Book of Kyng Arthur:*

The Unity of Malory's Morte Darthur by C. Moorman, 1965; *Romance and Chronicle: A Study of Malory's Prose Style* by P. J. C. Field, 1971; *Malory: Style and Vision in Le Morte Darthur* by Mark Lambert, 1975; *Malory's Morte Darthur* by Larry D. Benson, 1976.

*   *   *

Sir Thomas Malory's *Le Morte Darthur* is the basic source of our view of Lancelot, Arthur, and Gawain, of the Grail legend and of the Round Table. Although he did not invent most of his material, Malory abridged the monstrous bulk of the sources, simplified the narrative structure, modernized the tone and themes, and devised a coherent framework for these important tales. Camelot would not be one of the principal mythical settings of Western culture if Malory had not rescued the tales from extinction by organizing them in a vernacular prose version which focuses strongly on humanistic values, is couched in a graceful style, and is accessible to a large body of readers. The earlier romances glorified the epic virtues of *comitatus* and battlefield prowess as well as the medieval ideal of renunciation of worldly values. By focusing on individuals and their inner conflicts and placing high values on secular honor and political order, Malory modernized the basic themes. Particularly through his restructuring of the tales around the character of Lancelot, the best of worldly men, Malory transformed the tales for a modern reader. Malory's identity remains uncertain, but whoever he was, he did his work well.

William Caxton edited and printed the book he chose to call *Le Morte Darthur* because he thought of it as an exemplar: "that noble men may see and lerne the noble actes of chyvalrye, the jentyl and vertuous dedes that somme knyghtes used in tho dayes, by whyche they came to honour, and how they that were vycious were punysshed and ofte put to shame and rebuke." The work was known only in Caxton's version until W. F. Oakeshott discovered a fifteenth-century manuscript version in the Fellows' Library of Winchester College in 1934. Eugène Vinaver then edited the standard version, using the Caxton and Winchester texts.

The court of King Arthur is a central myth of human idealism, and it has occupied that place in Western thought for 500 years. Spenser, Tennyson, the Pre-Raphaelite painters, Sidney Lanier, John Steinbeck and others have drawn from the Malory canon, but none has rivalled the contribution he made. Because he combined material from French and Middle English romances, some scholars have dismissed him as a mere compiler, but a careful study of his work shows that in his abridging and organizing of the tales, Malory improved them and wove them into a pattern with rich symbolic threads. C. S. Lewis likened the result to a medieval cathedral. "Though every part of it was made by a man, the whole has rather grown than been made. Such things have a kind of existence that is almost midway between the works of art and those of nature."

One of the major techniques Malory used to gain coherence is the elimination of many minor characters and the reassignment of key adventures to knights he wished to emphasize. Thus some encounters undertaken by Gawain, Cador, and others in the sources are attributed in Malory to Lancelot. The mythic tale of the exiled nobleman who finds his heritage and proves his lineage, which is associated with Parzival among others in continental tales, is used to flesh out the story of Gareth, who is only an alliterative name in the sources.

Malory's small cast is headed by Merlin, the figures of the Tristram cycle, the families of King Lot and King Pellinore, the characters associated with the Grail, and Arthur, Guenevere, and Lancelot. He achieves a coordinating effect by using characters and incidents from one set of adventures to foreshadow or symbolize events and themes in another. He capitalizes on the similarities of incident between the Tristram story and the central love triangle to ennoble the character of Arthur the feuding between the families of Lot and Pellinore demonstrates a major weakness of the knightly bond which will be dissolved by the last campaign; the ethos of the Grail quest stands in stark contrast to the accepted behavior of merely adventurous questers.

Lancelot is the fulcrum on which Malory's work turns. His pre-eminence among knights is predicted before the founding of the Round Table, and he is the last of the major figures left alive. His trials and internal struggles are at the centre of many of the individual episodes and are the key to the major conflicts of the work. Sir Ector's lament over his body is an elegy for an entire era. Gawain's character suffers most from the advancement of Lancelot. In early stories Gawain was a noble knight and, as Arthur's nephew, foremost in the fellowship; in Malory's version Gawain is noted for violence and vengeance. He is noble only in his deathbed reconciliation with Lancelot.

Even Lancelot's failings are related to triumph. His illegitimate son, Galahad, is the finest of other-worldly knights and achieves completely the Grail quest Lancelot achieves partially. Though Lancelot slips back into the love affair with Guenevere after the Grail quest, he alone is able to heal Sir Urry, who can be healed only by the best knight in the world.

In the French account of the Grail quest, Lancelot is a symbol of sin. The hermits he meets deliver long and cruel lectures on his weakness and guilt. Malory omits the most condemnatory passages and focuses on instability as Lancelot's fatal weakness. His Lancelot has a limited vision of the Grail and develops spiritual awareness as he realizes the limitations of the earthly code of which he is the outstanding proponent. His failure to hold to that higher vision is a tragedy, but Lancelot remains a hero.

This careful development of Lancelot as a sympathetic and admirable character is related to the overall humanistic theme. In contrast to the renunciation-of-the-world theme of the French source, Malory emphasizes his view of chivalry as the closest man can come to a perfect society. Since he worked during the turbulent years of the War of the Roses, finishing in 1469–70, the reader can appreciate his enthusiasm for stability and idealism. His ideals are put forth in the oath sworn yearly by Arthur's knights:

> never to do outerage nothir morthir, and allwayes to fle treson, and to gyff mercy unto hym that askith mercy, uppon payne of forfiture [of their] worship and lordship of kynge Arthure for evirmore; and allwayes to do ladyes, damesels, and jantilwomen and wydowes [socour:] strengthe hem in hir rightes, and never to enforce them, uppon payne of dethe. Also that no man take no batayles in a wrongefull quarell for no love ne for no worldis goodis.

Malory saw the crumbling of that world not as a punishment of sin but as a tragedy brought on by instability, a flaw he found in his main character, Lancelot, and in the Englishmen of his own tempestuous time.

—Barbara M. Perkins

MEDWALL, Henry.   English.   Lived in the latter part of the 15th century; first positively known English dramatist; served as chaplain to John Morton, Archbishop of Canterbury, 1486–1500.

PUBLICATIONS

Plays

   Fulgens and Lucrece (produced 1497).   1515(?); edited by Glynne Wickham, in *English Moral Interludes,* 1976.

Nature.   1530(?); edited by J. S. Farmer, in *"Lost" Tudor Plays,* 1907.

Reading List: *Medwalls Fulgens and Lucres* by Hans Hecht, 1925; *The Tudor Interlude* by T. W. Craik, 1958; *The Staging of Plays Before Shakespeare* by Richard Southern, 1973.

*   *   *

Henry Medwall's two known plays (the story that he wrote a third which wearied Henry VIII is without foundation) are both two-part interludes designed as banquet entertainments at Cardinal Morton's palace. *Nature* is named after the opening speaker, but its central character is Man, and its pattern the typical morality one of temptation, fall, and restoration. Man, given Reason and Sensuality as his two companions, becomes governed by the latter, who introduces him to the seven deadly sins (under false names, Pride becoming Worship and so on). Reason, assisted by Shamefastness, reclaims him at the end of the first part, but in the second he reverts to his bad ways, until (off-stage) Age reconverts him to Reason. The plot is awkwardly managed, nothing being made of the impact of remorse on Man on either occasion; but the dialogue and stage movement are lively, and there are racy accounts of meetings with off-stage characters like Kate and Margery in taverns and brothels, while Nature's opening speech has some grandeur.

Fulgens and Lucres is far superior as drama, besides being more palatable to modern tastes because it employs neither allegory nor religious didacticism. It is a debate as to whether birth or merit constitutes a gentleman, the occasion being the wooing by two suitors of the contrary qualifications of the daughter (Lucretia) of a Roman senator (Fulgentius). The source is the English translation of a Latin prose *controversia* of 1428. To his borrowed plot Medwall has added a sub-plot involving two serving-men (A and B: their lack of proper names fosters the half-illusion that they are members of the audience joining in, which in turn fosters the further half-illusion that the events of the play are true and in the present). These attach themselves to the two rival suitors (carrying messages and making errors) and themselves become rivals for the love of Lucrece's waiting-maid, who makes them ridiculous. As involuntary parodists and foils, and as (often wrong-headed) commentators, they add a great deal to the play's substance as well as to its humour, and point towards later Shakespearean effects. Medwall uses mainly rhyme-royal stanzas for his serious monologues and dialogues, and tail-rhyme for his comic ones, though couplets also occur.

—T. W. Craik

RASTELL, John.   English.   Born in London c. 1475. Trained as a lawyer; entered Lincoln's Inn, London, 1502, and subsequently had a successful practice in London. Married Elizabeth More, sister of Sir Thomas More; one son. Printer in London, printing mainly legal books, from 1513; also served as Member of Parliament for Dunheved, Cornwall, 1529–36; involved in the religious controversies of the time from c. 1530: a convert to Protestantism; claimed in later life that his conversion had been the cause of the ruin of his legal practice and printing business. *Died in June 1536.*

PUBLICATIONS

Plays

>*The Nature of the Four Elements.* 1517–27(?); edited by Roger Coleman, 1971.
>*Terence in English* (translation of *Andria* by Terence). 1520(?).
>*Calisto and Melibea.* 1527(?); edited by H. W. Allen, 1908.
>*Gentleness and Nobility.* 1527(?); edited by K. W. Cameron, 1941.

Other

>*The Pastime of People.* 1529; edited by T. F. Dibdin, 1811.
>*A New Book of Purgatory.* 1530.

>Editor and Translator, *The Exposition of the Terms of the Laws of England.* 1526 (and later versions in English and French).
>Editor and Translator, *The Statutes.* 1527 (and later versions in English and French).

*   *   *

John Rastell's celebrity arises partly from his distinction as an early London publisher and humanist associate of Thomas More, his brother-in-law. As lawyer, Catholic turned Lutheran, member of the Reformation Parliament, and man of wide interests (contemporary science, social and legal reform, colonial exploration, the infant printing industry, amateur dramatics), he epitomizes the vigorous spirit of Henrician England. However, it is now customary also to credit him with an impressive group of original works, products of an independent and versatile mind. The disputative *New Boke of Purgatory*, if lacking the intellectual command, or the wit, range, and flexibility of More's religious polemics, attractively illuminates a theological controversy, while the discriminating spirit of modern historical criticism already informs Rastell's highly readable chronicle *Pastyme of People*, which as a model of fluent narrative prose deserves more respectful attention than it has usually received.

His three plays form a distinctive contribution to Tudor drama, in which field Rastell was probably something of an innovator, although essentially forensic motives led him to employ characters and situations to present information or advance debating-points rather than create intrinsically effective stage-images. In the incompletely preserved interlude *The Nature of the Four Elements* he adapts the form and techniques of the medieval religious morality to illustrate the principles and content of contemporary humanistic education: thus Nature, subjecting the student-hero Humanity to a course of instruction in Renaissance science and geography, is assisted by Studious Desire and Experience but hampered by the boastful vice Ignorance and the cheerfully disreputable Sensual Appetite who lures Humanity from his studies to the tavern. Although the lengthy didactic speeches and tame comic digressions compare unfavourably with those of Henry Medwall's earlier *Fulgens and Lucres*, and a dearth of psychological interest is also apparent, the piece remains a commendable attempt to extend the scope of the homiletic morality.

Gentylnes and Nobylyte depicts three "estates of the realm" (knight, merchant, and ploughman) engaging in debate over the relative importance of birth and behaviour in establishing social worth, but the argument becomes diffuse and characterization is thin, "discussion drama" being exploited more successfully by Rastell's son-in-law, John Heywood. More promising is *A new commodye in English*, adapted from the Spanish dialogue-romance *Celestina* and usually known as *Calisto and Meliboea*, which, in telling of the bawd Celestina's furtherance of the lovers' passionate liaison, breaks free from formal and ideological constraints to recount a human story. But Rastell evades the original's retributive dénouement in which the parties suffer violent deaths and substitutes a typical moral lecture; indeed, he rarely resists the opportunity to instruct or improve his auditors. Even when a genuinely dramatic development seems inevitable, artistic considerations are sacrificed to provide social or educational lessons void of theatrical vitality. Yet if Rastell failed to attain the invention, coherence, and finish of livelier playwrights of his age, his experiments are historically important, not least his *Terens in Englysh*, a pioneering version of Terence's romantic comedy, *Andria*.

—William M. Tydeman

SKELTON, John.   English. Born, probably in Yorkshire, c. 1460. Educated at Cambridge University (possibly at Peterhouse), B.A. possibly 1479; probably also at Oxford University (Poet Laureate of Oxford, 1488, and of Cambridge, 1505; Laureate, University of Louvain, 1492). At the end of his life claimed to be married to a woman in Diss, Norfolk, by whom he had had several children. Official court poet, 1488; tutor to Prince Henry, later King Henry VIII, 1494–1502; Orator Regius, 1512; enjoyed the patronage of Cardinal Wolsey and the Countess of Surrey (mother of the poet); ordained, 1498: Rector of Diss from 1502; satirized Wolsey in his verse, 1515–22. *Died 21 June 1529.*

PUBLICATIONS

Collections

Poetical Works, edited by Alexander Dyce.   2 vols., 1843; augmented by F. J. Child, 3 vols., 1856.
Complete Poems, edited by Philip Henderson.   1931; revised edition, 1964.
Poems, edited by R. S. Kinsman.   1969.

Verse

The Bowge of Court.   1499.
A Ballad of the Scottish King.   1513.
The Tunning of Elinor Rumming.   1521.
Speak Parrot.   1521.
A Goodly Garland or Chaplet of Laurel.   1523.
Divers Ballads and Ditties Salacious.   1527.
Against a Comely Coystrowne.   1527.
A Replication Against Certain Young Scholars.   1528.
Colin Clout.   1530.
Philip Sparrow.   1545.
Why Come Ye Not to Court?   1545.

Play

Magnificence.   1533; edited by J. Farmer, 1910.

Other

Certain Books.   1545.
Pithy, Pleasant, and Profitable Works, edited by John Stow.   1568.
Speculum Principis, edited by F. M. Salter, in *Speculum.*   1934.

Translator, *The Bibliotheca Historica of Diodorus Siculus,* edited by F. M. Salter and H.
    L. R. Edwards.   2 vols., 1956–57.

Reading List: *Skelton, Laureate* by William Nelson, 1939; *Skelton: Poet Laureate* by Ian A.
Gordon, 1943; *Skelton: The Life and Times of an Early Tudor Poet* by H. L. R. Edwards,
1949; *Skelton and Satire* by Arthur R. Heiserman, 1961; *Skelton: Contribution à l'Histoire
de la Prérenaissance Anglaise* by Maurice Pollet, 1962, translated by John Warrington, 1971;
La Poesia di Skelton by Edwige Schulte, 1963; *Skelton's Poetry* by Stanley E. Fish, 1965;
Skelton's "Magnyfycence" and the Cardinal Virtue Tradition by William O. Harris, 1965;
Skelton by Nan Cooke Carpenter, 1968.

*   *   *

Because he failed to understand the forces shaping early Renaissance England – the growth
of the modern monarchy, the need to reform the church from within, the development of
humanist scholarship and appreciation of classical prose style, the study of Greek – John
Skelton's verse seems to lash out intemperately, while paradoxically calling for temperance in
government, morality, and scholarship. This intemperance in the service of order gives his
verse its characteristic flavor, as various litigious or obsessed personae struggle to rebuke or
restrain others and, ultimately, themselves. The speakers so vigorously convey the passion
they ostensibly wish to control that it becomes their own: "He is so fyers and fell;/He rayles
and he ratis,/He calleth them doddypatis;/He grynnes and he gapys,/As it were jack napis./
Such a madde bedleme/For to rewle this reame" (*Why Come Ye Nat to Courte?*). The
pretense of quoting from one of Wolsey's tirades with "doddypatis" forces the speaker and
reader momentarily to experience Wolsey's anger. This mood of scarcely controlled
vituperation appears from the beginning of Skelton's career in the rhyme royal stanzas of the
elegy for the Earl of Northumberland (1489), which excoriates the Judas-like plotting of the
earl's retainers. Skelton's obsessiveness may stem from his sense of divine mission as heir to
both Apollo (or Skelton's favorite Latin poet Juvenal) and various Old Testament prophets.
    Skelton's obsessiveness dominates the brilliant *Bowge of Courte*, a variant of the medieval
dream vision. Drede, the appropriately named poet tempted aboard an imposing ship named
the Bowge of Courte (the wages or rewards of court), must finally leap overboard to escape
the lethal onslaught of the sinister allegorical figures who resent his competition. The fear and
other allegorized qualities that Drede tries to fight (Disceyte, Suspycyon) give the poem its
tone of unbearable obsession, lightened but not negated by Skelton's ironic humor. When
Drede awakes from his Kafkaesque nightmare, he is teasingly ambivalent about its meaning
and implies that life at court is not susceptible to rational control, a resolution less didactic
than in the traditional dream allegory.
    Though Skelton remained a brilliant manipulator of the iambic pentameter or looser four-
stress line in rhyme royal stanzas throughout his career, some time before the composition (c.
1505) of *Phyllyp Sparowe* he developed his signature verse form, the Skeltonic, a line of
generally two, sometimes three, accented and any number of unaccented syllables. The lines
exhibit structural alliteration, parallelism, and, most important, rhyme-runs of up to fourteen

lines, though couplets are frequent. The result, a rush of sound and sense in which individual lines count for little, suits his uncontrolled protagonists. Diverse theories have attempted to derive the form from origins as varied as the Latin sequence, the leonine hexameter, and Anglo-Saxon verse. That all these theories have some plausability suggests that the Skeltonic is the product of an eclectic imagination. Its closest rhythmical analogues are the verses of the 14th-century alliterative revival (the long four-beat lines tended to break in half); and the Skeltonic's combination of rhythm and rhyme parallels the stanzas of the Wakefield Master. Thus, within the body of medieval English verse with its fusion of native stress and continental syllabic traditions, there was a body of poetry resembling the Skeltonic. Because of these roots in the traditional rhythm of English verse, the Skeltonic can convey the illusion of direct speech and also, more surprisingly, multi-levelled irony, pathos, and expressionistic intensity.

Utilizing all these effects, the first part of *Phyllyp Sparowe* dramatizes a convent student's attempt to accept the loss of her pet sparrow, slain by the convent cat. Starting with tags from the Catholic Office for the Dead, the poem seems both a direct expression of the girl's uncomprehending grief, intensified by her desire for hyperbolic vengeance against all cats, and an elaborate parody of the mass, ironically inappropriate from the lips of a child. Occasionally, as with all Skelton personae, his voice fuses with that of his character to raise questions about the innocence the poem had been demonstrating: "To Jupyter I call,/Of heven emperyall,/That Phyllyp may fly/Above the starry sky,/To treade the prety wren/ That is our Ladyes hen./Amen, amen, amen!" After describing an elaborate bird mass and displaying her familiarity with the names of all the writers in the classical, medieval, and Renaissance pantheons (while protesting her lack of learning), young Jane accepts her loss by composing a Latin epitaph for the bird. The second part of the poem, "The Commendacyons," is a lengthy praise of Jane, as the poet presumably both stimulates and calms his own obsession with the erotic appeal of the adolescent girl. The poem, perhaps Skelton's finest, admirably controls the complex tones of the two voices.

Almost as successful is *The Tunnyng of Elinour Rummyng* (written c. 1517), an expressionistic picture of an alewife and her transcendantly vulgar female patrons. The genius of the poem is that, as the male speaker piles on detail after repetitive detail, his own involvement overcomes his disgust at the (doubly) infectious atmosphere: "Theyr thrust was so great/They asked never for mete/But 'Drynke, styll drynke,/And let the cat wynke!/Let us wasshe our gommes/From the drye crommes!' " The speaker's periodic pauses seem the exhaustion of real participation and prepare for the final: "For my fyngers ytche!/I have written to myche/Of this mad mummynge/Of Elinour Rummynge."

Some characteristic Skelton poems like "Against the Scottes" are primarily invectives and contributed to his reputation of boorish tastelessness and to the tradition of an unconventional private life preserved in the anonymous *Merie Tales by Maister Skelton* (1567). The most brilliant invective, "A Devoute Trentale" (for one of his less loved parishioners), celebrates in English and Latin Skeltonics the demise of John Jayberd, "incola de Dis" (a pun on the deceased's past and present domains), and epitomizes him wittily: "Senio confectus,/Omnibus suspectus,/Nemini dilectus,/Sepultus est emong the weedes:/ God forgyve him his mysdeedes." More indecent are the flytings against Garnesche, a court rival, which stress his low origins and unattractive person. These same traits appear later in the anti-Wolsey poems *Collyn Clout* and *Why Come Ye Nat to Courte?* which for many years established Skelton as a satirist and were often quoted in histories of the period.

The attack on Wolsey really begins in *Magnyfycence* (written 1515–16?), a generalized treatment of the danger to Henry VIII from advisors who advocate costly and immoral novelty. Perhaps the first secular morality, *Magnyfycence* focuses on wealth as the index to happiness, but its climactic stress on Prince Magnyfycence's conversion by Adversity, Goodhope, and Redress brings it close to the religious pattern. Despite metrical versatility and lively comic villains like Folly and Fancy, *Magnyfycence* is too long and undramatic to sustain much interest, and the protagonist displays too little suffering or insight to support his conversion and the theme of the work.

Collyn Clout (written 1521–22?) dramatizes, in the guise of attacks on ecclesiastical corruption, the speaker's struggle with his awareness of the futility of such attacks: "What can it avayle/To dryve forth a snayle/Or to make a sayle/Of a herynges tayle?/To ryme or to rayle,/Eyther for delyte/Or elles for despyte?" More ominous is his knowledge that the "polluted" language of criticism can threaten religion itself. The poem never convincingly resolves the protagonist's frustration but presents an arresting portrait of anxiety, like versified Nashe.

Speke, Parrot, a long poem in several parts, was especially popular in the 1930's when critics thought its allusiveness made it a kind of Renaissance *Waste Land*. The poem uses its pattern of Old Testament symbolism to mount an attack on Wolsey's abuses of power at home and abroad – "Hys wolvys hede, wanne, blo as lede,/gapythe over the crown" – a power stemming from Wolsey's inability to transcend his low origins, which make him treat human beings like merchandise: "So bolde a braggyng bocher, and flesshe sold so dere." Skelton's unilluminated conservatism shines through wittily in his attack on the impracticality of the New Learning: "But our Grekis theyr Greke so well have applyed,/That they cannot say in Greke, rydynge by the way,/'How, hosteler, fetche my hors a botell of hay.' " And the protagonist's final attempt to "speke now trewe and playne" makes clear that the poem's seeming complexity resulted from Parrot's caution about forthright utterance. As in all Skelton's supposed satires, he lacks the ability to select a meaningful detail that illuminates both a defect and its implied remedy though he compensates with a protagonist exaggerated to expressionistic proportions. Veering between an attack on Wolsey and the plight of the poet-reformer, the poem is a flawed but intriguing work.

Why Come Ye Nat to Courte?, a less complex dramatization of anger at Wolsey's one-man rule of church and state, succeeds primarily when the anger overreaches itself in finding outrageous and sometimes irrelevant expression. The bizarrely ingenious linking of Wolsey's sexual indiscretions (presumably the cause of his diseased eye) with his spiritual blindness, shocks, yet says nothing about the issues motivating the speaker's animosity. Like Collyn, the protagonist either maliciously or ignorantly attributes even Wolsey's possibly salutary reforms to willful malice or ignorance. Thus, the speaker exhibits the same outrageousness he attributes to Wolsey and undercuts any real satiric thrust.

"The Garlande of Laurell" (written 1523), a variant of the dream vision, seems more muted that most of Skelton's work, as the poet dreams of his ultimately triumphant evaluation at the Court of Fame. The poem's strength lies in its witty view of reputation, a prefiguring of the distinction between true and false fame in "Lycidas." One of the poem's envoys requests both a prebend and protection from Wolsey: "Inter spemque metum," a wish foreshadowing the theme of reconciliation in "A Replycacyon" (1527–29), which begins with a dedication to Wolsey and ends with an envoy stressing the poet's link with "hys noble grace,/That caused you to devyse/This lytel enterpryse." Despite the possible political motives for its composition, the poem, an attack on two Cambridge scholars forced to recant publicly their Lutheran activities, exhibits all the vigor and occasionally questionable taste of the flytings, as it excoriates the penitents. Like *Collyn Clout*, the poem concludes with a stress on the futility of writing verse designed to educate or improve its readers: "For be ye wele-assured/That frensy nor jelousy,/Nor heresy will ever dye." But the poem has insufficiently developed this theme to give the lines any impact. The force in "A Replycacyon," however self-serving its origins, that links it with the body of Skelton's best poetry is the continuing belief that "God maketh his habytacion/In poetes which excelles,/And sojourns with them and dwelles."

—Burton Kendle

SURREY, Earl of; Henry Howard.   English   Born, probably in Kenninghall, Norfolk, c.
1516; eldest son of Thomas Howard, Duke of Norfolk. Educated by the scholar John Clerke,
and possibly at Christ Church, Oxford. Married Lady Frances Vere in 1535. Cup-Bearer to
Henry VIII: accompanied Henry to France, 1532–33; Earl Marshal at the trial of Anne
Boleyn, 1536; Steward of Cambridge University, 1541; served with the army in Scotland,
1542; Field Marshal of the English army on the Continent, 1544; Commander at Boulogne,
1545–46, defeated at St. Etienne, and replaced by the Earl of Hertford, 1546; recalled to
England, and condemned and executed on charge of quartering royal arms. Knighted, 1536;
Knight of the Garter, 1541. *Died 21 January 1547.*

PUBLICATIONS

Collections

> *Poems,* edited by F. M. Padelford.   1920; revised edition, 1928.
> *Poems,* edited by Emrys Jones.   1964.

Verse

> *An Excellent Epitaph of Sir Thomas Wyatt.*   1542.
> *The Fourth Book of Virgil, Drawn into a Strange Metre.*   1554.
> *Certain Books of Virgil's Aenaeis.*   1557; edited by F. H. Ridley, 1963.
> *Songs and Sonnets* (Tottel's miscellany; 40 poems by Surrey).   1557.

Reading List: *Surrey* by Edwin Casady, 1938; *The Elizabethan Love Sonnet* by J. W. Lever,
1959; *Two Tudor Portraits: Surrey and Lady Katherine Grey* by Hester W. Chapman, 1960;
" 'Love that doth raine': Surrey's Creative Imitation" by W. O. Harris, in *Modern Philology*
66, 1969.

*   *   *

When Surrey's poems were printed alongside Wyatt's in Tottel's miscellany in 1557, his
were given pride of place because they suited the taste of the time and the compiler's ideas of
correctness. Nearly all the critics during the next three centuries agreed that Surrey was
Wyatt's superior, largely because of the smoothness of his versification. In the present
century, paradoxically because of the renewed interest in Donne, Wyatt's reputation has
grown steadily and Surrey's has as steadily declined. Yet, although Wyatt is doubtless the
better poet, acknowledged by Surrey as his master, the pupil is by no means negligible.
    Much of his work can be seen as a continuation of Wyatt's. Wyatt, for example, had
versified the Penitential Psalms, setting them in a narrative framework of David's love for
Bathsheba. Surrey at the end of his short life, when his enemies were plotting against him,
wrote verse paraphrases of five chapters of *Ecclesiastes* and of four Psalms. It is easy to see
why he chose Psalm 55: "My foes they bray so loud, and eke threpe on so fast,/Buckled to do
me scathe, so is their malice bent." Surrey also followed Wyatt in translating a number of
Petrarch's sonnets, sometimes diverging from the originals (as Wyatt had done), e.g., "The
soote season that bud and blome furth brings," but more usually sticking close to the Italian.
His versification was more musical than Wyatt's and he would not have rhymed "suffer"
with "banner" as Wyatt did. Yet Wyatt succeeded in making original poems, as when he
adapted a Petrarchan sonnet to express his grief on the execution of his friend and patron,

Thomas Cromwell; and Surrey's generally read like translations. The two poets can be directly compared in one instance, since they translated the same sonnet, Wyatt's "The longe love that in my thought doeth harbar" and Surrey's "Love that doth raine and live within my thought." Wyatt has revitalised the imagery; but Surrey's is more immediately accessible and closer to the original.

Surrey, however, was able sometimes to use translation as a means of self-expression, especially his feeling for nature, as in the opening of one of the sonnets:

> Alas, so all thinges nowe doe holde their peace,
> Heaven and earth disturbed in no thing;
> The beastes, the ayer, the birds their song doe cease;
> The nightes chare the starres aboute dothe bring.
> Calme is the sea, the waves worke lesse and lesse;
> So am not I, whom love alas doth wring.

The other love poems are written in various styles. Eight of them, like most of the Biblical paraphrases, are written in Poulter's Measure – a metre in which Wyatt had contrived to write the most unreadable of his poems. Most of Surrey's, it must be confessed, are somewhat wooden, but in one or two he scores a modest success by his use of simple and unaffected language. One of the best – supposed to be spoken by a woman – begins:

> Good ladies, you that have your pleasure in exyle,
> Stepp in your foote, come take a place, and mourne with me awhyle;
> And such as but their lords do sett but lytle pryce,
> Let them sitt still, it stills them not what chaunce come on the dyce.

One of Surrey's love poems, partially translated, is in *terza rima*, the form used by Wyatt in his satires and psalms. But the ones that have worn best, to judge by their frequent appearance in modern anthologies, are the short lyrics in stanza form. They were not intended, as Wyatt's obviously were, to be set to music; but they are closer in spirit to English songs than to his Italian models. One of them, expressing the feelings of a wife whose husband is on the seas, contains two echoes from Serafino but they have been assimilated into the very English poem:

> When other lovers in armes acrosse
> Rejoyce their chief delight,
> Drowned in teares to mourne my losse
> I stand the bitter night
> In my window, where I may see
> Before the windes how the cloudes flee.
> Lo, what a mariner love hath made me!

The same poem ends with the colloquial line: "Now he comes, will he come? alas, no, no!"

It is important to remember that Surrey was just thirty when he died, and that much of his best verse was written on subjects other than love. The poem he wrote in Windsor Castle in 1537 effectively contrasts his imprisonment with the happier years he spent there as a companion to the Duke of Richmond. Perhaps his finest poem is the elegy on Wyatt, written in 1542, in which his admiration for his mentor's integrity, courage, and piety brings out a reflection of those qualities in himself. It is perhaps the finest English elegy before "Lycidas." The satirical poem on London, written after his arrest for riotous behaviour, shows that alongside his pride and piety was a lack of self-control; but his translations of Horace and Martial, written in a direct and masculine style, show that his beliefs and ideals, if not always his conduct, were approximating to those of Wyatt.

It is not known when his translation of the *Aeneid* II and IV was written: it was his most influential, and probably his most important, work. It owes something to Gavin Douglas's translation, but unlike that it is written in blank verse – apparently the first to be written in English. He realised that rhyme would give a wrong impression of Virgil's epic. Surrey's verse is usually end-stopped, and his translation lacks narrative drive; but he manages the speeches effectively and he has many felicitous phrases.

His success with the speeches was the main reason why Elizabethan dramatists, unlike the French, avoided rhymed tragedies, and why Milton chose blank verse for *Paradise Lost* instead of the stanzaic form of Spenser, Tasso, and Ariosto, or the couplets of Cowley's biblical epic. Surrey was also responsible in some of his sonnets for the invention of the English form (three quatrains and a couplet) which Shakespeare gratefully followed.

—Kenneth Muir

UDALL, Nicholas. English. Born in Hampshire in 1505. Educated at Winchester College (scholar), 1517–20; Corpus Christi College, Oxford, admitted a scholar 1520, B.A. 1524, probationer-fellow 1524, M.A. 1534. Tutor at Corpus Christi College from 1524; Headmaster of Eton College, 1534–41; Vicar of Braintree, Essex, 1537–44; Prebend at Windsor, 1551, and Rector of Calborne, Isle of Wight, 1553; appointed playwriter to Queen Mary, 1554; Headmaster of Westminster School, London, 1554–56. *Died* (buried) *23 December 1556.*

PUBLICATIONS

Plays

  Ralph Roister Doister (produced 1553?).   1566(?); edited by G. Scheurwegh, 1939.
  Respublica (produced 1553).   Edited by J. P. Collier, in *Illustrations of English Literature*, 1866; edited by W. W. Greg, 1952.
  Jack Juggler (produced ?).   1563; edited by E. L. Smart and W. W. Greg, 1937.
  Jacob and Esau (produced ?).   1568; edited by J. Crow and F. P. Wilson, 1956.

Other

  Flowers for Latin Speaking, from Terence.   1533.
  Apothegms, from Erasmus.   1542.
  The Paraphrase of Erasmus upon the New Testament.   1548.
  A Discourse Concerning the Lord's Supper, from P. M. Vermigh.   1550(?).

  Translator, *Compendiosa Totius Anatomie Delineatio* (in English), by Thomas Geminus.   1553; revised edition, 1559.

Reading List: Introduction by C. D. O'Malley to *Compendiosa*, 1959.

*   *   *

Nicholas Udall is the known author of only one extant play, *Ralph Roister Doister*, and of one lost one, *Ezechias* (acted 1564, but possibly Henrician in date and polemical in matter). He has been credited with *Thersites, Jack Juggler, Respublica,* and *Jacob and Esau*; of these the last three are more likely to be his than the first, both for their Terentian structure and for their versification and diction (especially the last two). Writing for boy actors, he reflects the new interest in classical comedy (he published a Terentian Latin-English phrase-book, *Flowers for Latin Speaking*) as studied in schools. The models of *Ralph Roister Doister,* Terence's *Eunuchus* and *Miles Gloriosus,* gave Udall his comic duo of braggart lover and flattering parasite, here called Ralph Roister-Doister and Matthew Merrygreek (nearly all the names alliterate). The braggart's wooing proceeds from one disaster to another: his love-tokens are refused, his commissioned love-letter ruined by his own mispunctuation, his assault on his intended wife's house repulsed by her and her servants with kitchen armaments – to the barely concealed enjoyment of Merrygreek, who at one point reads a mock-requiem over his despairing patron. After a brief misunderstanding between the lady and her accepted suitor, the latter is convinced that Roister-Doister's courtship was without her encouragement, and a general feast ends the play.

Respublica (which survives in a manuscript stating that it was played by boys before Mary I) is a political morality in Terentian technique, showing how Avarice and his subordinate vices Insolence, Oppression, and Adulation take false names in order to exploit Respublica and oppress her rustic servant People under the guise of reforming their estate until Nemesis (identified with the Queen) exposes them. *Jacob and Esau* treats the biblical story in the manner of the humanist religious drama, equipping the main characters with neighbours and with household servants who would be at home in *Ralph Roister Doister.* All three plays are divided into acts and scenes, introduce their characters by Terentian techniques, and develop the action systematically to a crisis and catastrophe. They are written in freely rhythmical couplets and all contain songs. The dialogue is idiomatic and there is plenty of English local colour, even in the biblical play. This last point also applies to *Jack Juggler,* but its plot is from Plautus (his *Amphitryon*), not from Terence, it is undivided into acts and scenes, and it contains no songs. (*Thersites,* loosely based on a neo-classical dialogue, is closer akin to the style of earlier than middle sixteenth-century drama.)

—T. W. Craik

VAUX, Thomas; 2nd Baron Vaux of Harrowden. English. Born in Harrowden, Northamptonshire, in 1510; eldest son of the first Baron Vaux; succeeded to the barony, 1523. Educated at Cambridge University. Married Elizabeth Cheney; two sons and two daughters. Served with Cardinal Wolsey in France, 1527, and with Henry VIII, in Calais and Boulogne, 1532; attended the House of Lords, 1530–55; Captain of the Isle of Jersey until 1536. Knight of the Bath, 1533. *Died in October 1556.*

PUBLICATIONS

Collections

Poems, edited by Larry P. Vonalt. 1960.

*   *   *

Thomas, Lord Vaux, is of the period of Wyatt and Surrey, and is a good example of the "courtly maker" of the day. Though only fifteen poems definitely ascribed to him have survived, Vaux has enjoyed a considerable posthumous reputation. His work appeared in the most popular Elizabethan anthologies, two poems in Tottel's *Miscellany*, the rest in *The Paradise of Dainty Devices*. Many were set to music; two had the additional exposure of the stage, most notably "The Aged Lover Renounceth Love," three muddled stanzas of which are sung by the gravedigger in *Hamlet*. Praised by Puttenham in 1586 for "the facillitie of his meetre" and the precision of his style, Vaux has held the respect of critics for his simplicity, polish, and evident religious sincerity. In 1939 Yvor Winters claimed Vaux as "a distinguished representative" of the native plain style, and in that guise he has experienced a mild but durable revival over the past several decades.

Vaux wrote on amatory and penitential subjects. Despite an occasional fine line or image – e.g., "Like as the hart that lifteth up his ears/To hear the hound ..." or "The days be long that hang upon desert" – some of his love poems fail to cohere under the burden of the miscellaneous conceits with which they are adorned. Others are successfully held together by clever chains of imagery or are redeemed by elegance and wit. The mysterious obscurity of three poems on false blame hints of a particularity unusual in Vaux, but a particularity that rather cripples than invigorates their emotional power. In "The Assault of Cupid" Vaux turns to the richer vein of medieval love allegory, creating something of a spoof by substituting for the stately interplay of abstractions a spirited account of modern warfare, complete with pikemen and guns that fill the air with smoke.

A different medieval flavor distinguishes "The Aged Lover," which not only details the usual reminders of death but also confronts, as in a mirror, the poet's aging self: gray hair, bald pate, wrinkles, cough, bent spine, and failing poetic inspiration. To this harrowing meditation on the passage of time Vaux adds his favorite moral theme of guilt and repentance for past and not yet relinquished follies. But he is not always unremittingly sober in the moral poems. "Of a Contented Mind," for example, elaborates a bitter Stoic thought, only to conclude with a wink, "I can be well content/The sweetest time of all my life to deem in thinking spent."

A master of technique, Vaux expressed that mastery by working within the confines of conventional themes and genres. In his poems one never hears a distinct voice, such as that of Wyatt, chafing against traditional values and responses; rather, Vaux offers the impersonal, classic voice of the tradition itself, in its pure, controlled, and full expression.

—William E. Sheidley

WAKEFIELD MASTER.

PUBLICATIONS

Plays

The Wakefield Pageants in the Towneley Cycle, edited by A. C. Cawley. 1958.

Reading List: "The Craftsmanship of the Wakefield Master" by H-J. Diller, in *Anglia 83*, 1965; Introduction by M. Rose to *The Wakefield Mystery Plays*, 1961; *The English Mystery Plays* by R. Woolf, 1972; *The Construction of the Wakefield Cycle* by John Gardner, 1974.

*   *   *

The Wakefield Master was a man of exceptional dramatic skill who wrote and revised parts of the Towneley Cycle of mystery plays in the first half of the fifteenth century. His highly original style is characterised by a) local allusions, referring to places in the neighbourhood of Wakefield, Yorkshire; b) vivid language, utilising proverbs, colloquialisms, vulgarisms, and sometimes blasphemy; c) frequent anachronism; d) a fondness for developing non-biblical material, particularly folktales; e) extensive use of a unique nine-line stanza of varying line length, rhyming aaaabcccb with internal rhyme in the first four. A. C. Cawley in *The Wakefield Pageants* further adds "a lively use of gesture and action, an outspoken criticism of contemporary abuses, a bold rehandling of secular material for comic purposes, and an unusual skill in characterization."

The extent of his work has to be inferred on stylistic grounds. Of the thirty-two plays in the Towneley manuscript, five complete plays − *Noah* (3), *First Shepherds' Play* (12), *Second Shepherds' Play* (13), *Herod* (16), and *The Buffeting* (21) − can with conviction be assigned to him as they are written entirely in the nine-line stanza. Plays 2, 20, 22, 23, 24, 27, 29, and 30 make some use of this stanza, and probably reflect a reworking of older material. This second group has verbal and thematic parallels with the first, particularly in play 2 (*The Killing of Abel*), which is reckoned to be largely, if not entirely, the Wakefield Master's work, despite the fact that it contains only one stanza of characteristic Wakefield form.

The Wakefield Master's technique is most clearly demonstrated by comparison with the York, Chester, and *Ludus Coventriae* plays on the same subjects (see H-J. Diller). Noah's building of the ark, for instance, clearly presented a problem and a challenge to the mystery play authors. In the York *Building of the Ark* Noah simply describes his actions; in the Chester *Deluge* the speeches and the actions are stylised; in *Ludus Coventriae* Noah goes offstage and returns with the ark fully constructed; but the Wakefield Master's technique is to intersperse Noah's commentary on his solitary work with frequent pleas to the Almighty ("Unless God help ..."), physical reactions ("Now I'll throw off my gown and work in my tunic ..."), complaints ("My back will break, I think ..."), and psychological reactions ("It is better made than I could have thought ..."). The dramatic potential is thus more fully realised.

Whereas in many of the mystery plays characters simply enact the facts of a well-established narrative, the *dramatis personae* of the Master's plays have motivation and psychological realism, so that we often witness the evolution of an idea in the context of external events. We recognise in Cain, for example, a brooding and irrational grievance developing against Abel; we recognise in Herod a dangerous combination of temporal power and spiritual weakness through which he is steered towards his desperate plan to slaughter the Innocents; we see in Caiaphas the flame of anger growing fiercer as Jesus maintains his rigid silence in the face of his accusers.

The Wakefield Master's dramatic skill is nowhere more clearly shown than in his best-known work, *The Second Shepherds' Play*, apparently an alternative to *The First Shepherds' Play* which is different in all but the formal biblical features and in the general characterisation of the Shepherds themselves. Mak's elaborate scheme to steal a sheep provides a good plot, and the hiding of the animal in a cradle is clearly a bold parody of the birth of Christ, "the lamb of God." The audience is involved by reference to contemporary conditions, local places, and possibly local personages: there is good balance between scenes, with subtle movement from one to the next: there are humour and tension, as when the Third Shepherd's tenderness in presenting a gift to the supposed "child" in its cradle results in the discovery of the stolen sheep. All the same, the visit of the Shepherds to the Christ Child in the stable is simple and dignified.

Praise of the Wakefield Master, though extensive, has been tempered by some adverse criticism. The charge to which he is most susceptible is that his extensive use of secular material obscures the essential doctrinal themes of his plays; however, it is possible that the subjects on which he wrote (especially Noah, the Shepherds, and Herod) had already become established points of farce and light relief in the cycles as a whole.

—G. A. Lester

———————

WYATT, Sir Thomas.   English.   Born at Allington Castle, Kent, in 1503. Educated at St. John's College, Cambridge, matriculated 1515, B.A. 1518, M.A. 1520. Married the Hon. Elizabeth Brooke in 1520 (separated, 1526). Courtier of King Henry VIII: Clerk of the King's Jewels, 1524–31; sent on a diplomatic mission to France, 1526; accompanied Sir John Russell, Ambassador to the Papal Court, 1527; Marshal of Calais Castle, 1528–32; Justice of the Peace, Essex, 1532; Privy Councillor, 1533; imprisoned in connection with charges of adultery with Anne Boleyn, then pardoned, 1536; knighted, and appointed Sheriff of Kent, 1537; Ambassador to Spain and to the Emperor Charles V, 1537–39; on embassy in France and Holland, 1539–40; charged with treason, as an ally of Cromwell, imprisoned in the Tower, tried and acquitted, 1541; granted lands at Lambeth, London, by the king, 1541, and appointed High Steward of the king's manor at Maidstone, Kent, 1542. *Died 11 October 1542.*

PUBLICATIONS

Collections

    Collected Poems, edited by Kenneth Muir and Patricia Thomson.   1969.
    Collected Poems, edited by Joost Daalder.   1975.

Verse

    Certain Psalms Commonly Called the VII Penitential Psalms, edited by J. Harington.   1549.
    Songs and Sonnets (Tottel's miscellany; 97 poems by Wyatt).   1557.
    Unpublished Poems by Wyatt and His Circle, edited by Kenneth Muir.   1961.

Other

    Translator, *Plutarch's Book of the Quiet of Mind.*   1528; edited by C. R. Baskervill, 1931.

Reading List: *Humanism and Poetry in the Early Tudor Period* by H. A. Mason, 1959; *Wyatt* by Sergio Baldi, 1961; *Life and Letters of Wyatt* by Kenneth Muir, 1963; *Wyatt and His Background* by Patricia Thomson, 1964, and *Wyatt: The Critical Heritage,* edited by Thomson, 1974; *The Canon of Wyatt's Poetry* by Richard Harrier, 1975.

*   *   *

Unfortunately for modern readers, some aspects of Sir Thomas Wyatt's poetry remain problematic for lack of sure scholarly knowledge. Although many of his lyrics may have been set to music, only one contemporary accompaniment has been discovered; and the principles of Tudor scansion and pronunciation have by no means been finally ascertained. Such matters are of more than academic interest, for they have a bearing on the vexed question of Wyatt's metrical technique, which in its turn must affect our estimate of his poetic stature. Some of Wyatt's importance, moreover, is primarily historical. In translating from a number of Italian originals (including Ariosto and Petrarch) he regained for English poetry something of the cosmopolitan scope it had enjoyed in Chaucer's time. In pioneering the development of the English sonnet, he carried out a labour whose significance is at once apparent, even if later sonneteers such as Sidney and Spenser based their work less on the foundations laid by Wyatt than on a fresh recourse to foreign models.

A critical estimate of Wyatt's poetry must concentrate, however, on its intrinsic merits. In this respect the sonnets are much less important than the lyrics or "ballets," of which there are over 120, and whose stanzaic form is richly varied. It is in these lyrics, for the most part brief and song-like in construction, that we find displayed Wyatt's characteristic gifts; and here there is less evidence of the metrical uncertainty which is apt to interfere with our enjoyment of the more formal pieces. The following lines, from one of Wyatt's Petrarchan versions, illustrate the irregularities which typically beset the sonnets:

> My plesaunt dayes they flete away and passe,
> But daily yet the ill doeth chaunge into the wours;
> And more then the halfe is runne of my cours.

The most ingenious reader cannot make these last two lines scan. And the argument that such lines represent a deliberate departure from the iambic norm meets with the justifiable retort that a norm is precisely what Wyatt fails to establish. He never confidently controls either the stress-pattern or the syllabic foundation of his verse, and the resultant uncertainty undermines many of his efforts after rhythmic delicacy. But we can not dismiss the sonnets out of hand, for even here there are numerous brief passages suggestive of Wyatt's originality, and couched in his graphic and forceful idiom; and occasionally, as in the Petrarchan translation "My galy, charged with forgetfulness," an entire poem is sustained at this level, to memorable effect.

Apart from the sonnets, we must mention briefly a number of other works, including a set of penitential Psalms and three Satires, two Horatian and one original. This latter gives us an attractive picture of Wyatt sitting "in Kent and Christendome/Emong the muses where I rede and ryme."

It is in the ballets, however, as we have suggested, that Wyatt is at his best. The most famous of these − "They fle from me that sometyme did me seke," "Ons as methought fortune me kissed," "My lute awake!" − are written in a poetic medium capable of expressing a wide variety of feeling and of achieving cadences of haunting gravity: "But all is torned thorough my gentilnes/Into a straunge fasshion of forsaking." Even the less inspired of the short lyrics have an ease of movement which avoids all suggestion of the mechanical. The formal conventions − the use, for instance, of refrain − are turned to the poet's own purpose, just as the conventional ethics and rhetoric of courtly love are charged with a personal urgency which gives them fresh life.

For the achievement of Wyatt's best lyrics is not primarily technical. Technique is the servant: the poems are controlled by a rare dramatic and psychological intelligence whose insights transcend the limitations of the particular code of love in whose context Wyatt wrote. Although the situations are familiar – the lover communes with himself about the progress of his suit, or reproaches his mistress for her cruelty, or proclaims his own fidelity – their treatment often involves an unexpected emotional complexity. Consider, for instance, the irony and compassion implicit in the lines beginning "There was never nothing more me payned," where the poet upbraids himself for his hardheartedness, while recognising that he will undoubtedly continue to give his mistress cause for her grief. And where the feeling is simpler, it may be given superbly direct expression: "And wilt thou leave me thus?/Say nay, say nay, for shame...."

The lyrics we have mentioned, and others like them, are unmistakably Wyatt's: no-one else could have written them, and English poetry would be the poorer without them. It is this personal and unique voice which speaks to us still today, and this, for the general reader if not for the specialist, must outweigh considerations of Wyatt's historical importance. Wyatt is one of the enduring love-poets of the language.

—James Reeves

NOTES ON CONTRIBUTORS

ALEXANDER, M. J. Lecturer in English, University of Stirling, Scotland. Author of *The Earliest English Poems*, 1966, and *Beowulf*, 1973. **Essay:** Beowulf Poet.

CRAIK, T. W. Professor of English, University of Durham. Author of *The Tudor Interlude*, 1958, and *The Comic Tales of Chaucer*, 1964. Joint General Editor of *The Revels History of Drama in the English Language*, and editor of plays by Massinger, Marlowe, and Shakespeare. **Essays:** Henry Medwall; Nicholas Udall.

GILL, Roma. Member of the Department of English, University of Sheffield. Editor of *The Plays of Christopher Marlowe*, 1971, *William Empson: The Man and His Work*, 1974, and of works by Middleton and Tourneur. **Essay:** John Bale.

KENDLE, Burton. Associate Professor of English, Roosevelt University, Chicago. Author of articles on D. H. Lawrence, John Cheever, and Chekhov. **Essay:** John Skelton.

LESTER, G. A. Lecturer in English Language and Medieval Literature, University of Sheffield. Author of *The Anglo-Saxons*, 1976. **Essays:** Cynewulf; John Heywood; Wakefield Master.

LINDSAY, Maurice. Director of the Scottish Civic Trust, Glasgow, and Managing Editor of *The Scottish Review*. Author of several books of verse, the most recent being *Walking Without an Overcoat*, 1977; plays; travel and historical works; and critical studies, including *Robert Burns: The Man, His Work, The Legend*, 1954 (revised, 1968), *The Burns Encyclopedia*, 1959 (revised, 1970), and *A History of Scottish Literature*, 1977. Editor of the Saltire Modern Poets series, several anthologies of Scottish writing, and works by Sir Alexander Gray, Sir David Lyndsay, Marion Angus, and John Davidson. **Essays:** William Dunbar; Sir David Lyndsay.

LYLE, A. W. Lecturer in English, University of Sheffield. **Essay:** Alexander Barclay.

MacLAINE, Allan H. Professor of English, University of Rhode Island, Kingston. Author of *The Student's Comprehensive Guide to the Canterbury Tales*, 1964, *Robert Fergusson*, 1965, and of articles on Burns. **Essay:** Gavin Douglas.

McDIARMID, Matthew P. Member of the Department of English, University of Aberdeen, Scotland. Author of articles on Scots writers for the *Scottish Historical Review* and other periodicals. Editor of works by John Barbour, James I, and Robert Fergusson. **Essays:** John Barbour; Blind Hary; Sir Richard Holland.

MITCHELL, Jerome. Professor of English, University of Georgia, Athens. Fulbright Guest Professor, University of Bonn, 1972–73; former editor of *South Atlantic Bulletin*. Author of *Thomas Hoccleve: A Study in Early 15th-Century English Poetic*, 1968, and *The Walter Scott Operas*, 1977. **Essay:** Thomas Hoccleve.

MUIR, Kenneth.   Professor Emeritus of English Literature, University of Liverpool; Editor of *Shakespeare Survey,* and Chairman, International Shakespeare Association. Author of many books, including *The Nettle and the Flower,* 1933; *King Lear,* 1952; *Elizabethan Lyrics,* 1953; *John Milton,* 1955; *Shakespeare's Sources,* 1957; *Shakespeare and the Tragic Pattern,* 1959; *Shakespeare the Collaborator,* 1960; *Introduction to Elizabethan Literature,* 1967; *The Comedy of Manners,* 1970; *The Singularity of Shakespeare,* 1977; *Shakespeare's Comic Sequence,* 1978. Editor of several plays by Shakespeare, and of works by Wyatt and Middleton; translator of five plays by Racine. **Essay:** Henry Howard, Earl of Surrey.

NORTON-SMITH, J.   Reader in English Language and Literature, University of Dundee, Scotland; Editor of *Reading Medieval Studies* and General Editor of Brill's Medieval and Renaissance Authors series. Author of *Six Poems and Six Drawings* (with Fritz Janschka), 1972, and *Geoffrey Chaucer,* 1974. Editor of *Poems* by John Lydgate, 1966, *The Kingis Quair* by James I, 1971, and *The Quare of Jelusy,* 1975. **Essays:** James I, King of Scotland; John Lydgate.

PEARSALL, Derek.   Professor, Centre for Medieval Studies, University of York. Author of *Gower and Lydgate,* 1969, *Lydgate,* 1970, and *Old English and Middle English Poetry,* 1977. Editor of *Medieval Literature and Civilisation* (with R. A. Waldron), 1969, *Landscapes and Seasons of the Medieval World* (with Elizabeth Salter), 1973, and *Piers Plowman* by William Langland, 1978. **Essays:** Gawain Poet; John Gower; William Langland; Layamon.

PERKINS, Barbara M.   Director of Writing Improvement, Humanities Program, Eastern Michigan University, Ypsilanti. **Essay:** Sir Thomas Malory.

REEVES, James.   Author of more than 50 books, including verse (*Collected Poems,* 1974), plays, and books for children; critical works include *The Critical Sense,* 1956, *Understanding Poetry,* 1965, *Commitment to Poetry,* 1969, *Inside Poetry* (with Martin Seymour-Smith), 1970, and *The Reputation and Writings of Alexander Pope,* 1976. Editor of many collections and anthologies, and of works by D. H. Lawrence, Donne, Clare, Hopkins, Robert Browning, Dickinson, Coleridge, Graves, Swift, Johnson, Marvell, Gray, Whitman, and others; translator of fairy tales. Died, 1978. **Essay:** Sir Thomas Wyatt.

SCOBIE, Brian W. M.   Member of the Faculty, School of English, University of Leeds. **Essay:** Robert Henryson.

SHEIDLEY, William E.   Associate Professor of English, University of Connecticut, Storrs. Co-Editor of the journal *Children's Literature,* 1974–77. Author of articles on Marlowe, George Turbervile, Barnabe Googe, and Shakespeare in *Concerning Poetry, Journal of English and Germanic Philology, Studies in Philology,* and *Modern Language Quarterly.* **Essay:** Thomas Vaux.

TRAVERSI, Derek A.   Professor of English Literature, Swarthmore College, Pennsylvania. Author of *An Approach to Shakespeare,* 1938 (revised, 1968); *Shakespeare: The Last Phase,* 1954; *Shakespeare: From Richard II to Henry V,* 1957; *Shakespeare: The Roman Plays,* 1963; *T. S. Eliot: The Longer Poems,* 1976. **Essay:** Geoffrey Chaucer.

TYDEMAN, William M.   Senior Lecturer in English, University College of North Wales, Bangor. Author of *The Theatre in the Middle Ages,* 1978, and of the chapter on the earlier 16th century in *Year's Work in English Studies,* 1971–74. Editor of *English Poetry 1400–1580,* 1970, and of casebooks on Wordsworth and Coleridge. **Essays:** Stephen Hawes; John Rastell.

i